Justin Trudeau, Judicial Corruption and the Supreme Court of Canada:

Aliens and Archons in Our Midst

by Peter Tremblay

Agora Books

Agora Books
Ottawa, Canada

Justin Trudeau, Judicial Corruption and the Supreme Court of Canada: Aliens and Archons in Our Midst

c. 2019 by Peter Tremblay

Agora Books
P.O. Box 24191
300 Eagleson Road
Kanata, Ontario K2M 2C3

Agora Books is a self-publishing agency for authors that was launched by The Agora Cosmopolitan which is a registered not-for-profit corporation.

ISBN: 978-1-927538-49-4

Printed in Canada

Contents

Preface

*J*ustin Trudeau, Judicial Corruption and the Supreme Court of Canada: Aliens *and Archons in Our Midst* goes beyond the well-publicized and alleged corruption revealed by former Minister of Justice and Attorney General of Canada Jody Wilson-Raybould into alleged alien manipulation. Such manipulation has been reported by different reliable sources, including Dr. Michael Salla and former Canadian Defence Minister Paul Hellyer.

In this book, Peter Tremblay uses judicial proceedings involving the Carby-Samuels case to substantiate the apparent existence of alien manipulation through strategically placed "Archons".

It was John Lash who had documented in Metahistory.org ancient Pagan Gnostic insights of the Archons as an "artificial intelligence" which manifests from inorganic entities in a lower-dimensional cosmic realm of demons. Archons is a collusion of manipulative aliens and humans in elite positions of power that have sold themselves out to aliens identified by Dr. Michael Salla.

Are we, as humans, still yet to come in contact with other sentient life forms in our universe, as the elites would have us believe?

There are mountains of evidence that this is simply not the case. In this book, veteran investigative journalist Peter Tremblay, who has campaigned in support of former Canadian Defence Minister Paul Hellyer, brings together journalistic reports on a coordinated and apparent conspiracy among manipulative aliens and their Archon fronts. Such Archons appear to operate as "fifth columns" embedded within the police, the judiciary, and other institutions of governance in a manner similar to the way that terrorists can operate "sleeper cells" within various organizations.

The operations of aliens through their Archons are revealed through judicial proceedings in the Carby-Samuels case that have been documented by various investigative journalists who have worked with Peter Tremblay. In this book, Tremblay documents a path of alien manipulation and intrigue in relation to Dezrin Carby-Samuels, along with her husband Horace Carby-Samuels, and the efforts of their son to seek his mother's liberation from these apparent Archons.

Ms. Carby-Samuels has been subjected to apparent forcible confinement under an apparent regressive alien which has resulted in her not being able to walk, talk, or write anymore.

Peter Tremblay has worked for many years in government, including ministers 'offices, with all major Canadian political parties, and has observed a pattern of manipulation that seems to subvert our human identity as beings of love, empathy, and peace into a context of corruption through a system of justice that this book documents.

As Tremblay reveals, the corruption which played out in the Canadian justice system through the SNC-Lavalin scandal between the offices of the Prime Minister and the Minister of Justice is only the tip of the iceberg. Indeed, there exists a sea of apparent corruption which undermines the desire of not only Canadians but all of humanity to pursue a society based upon social justice, ethics, due process, and the rule of law.

It is therefore totally unconstructive to believe that one leader or even a single political party will result in the kind of change that voters seek.

As the plight of Dezrin Carby-Samuels shows, the corruption that manifests in political systems and throughout society which results in social injustices is the product of systematized orchestration by manipulative aliens.

Dezrin Carby-Samuels and other humans now face what might be the greatest threat to human sovereignty. This threat is not climate change, but something referred to by Dr. Michael Salla in his research of alien activity as "exopolitics." It is an apparent attempt by Archons to transform humanity from a society of beings with free will into managed entities under systematized corruption in what has been popularly referred to as the "Mandela Effect."

It is apparent that our world has little hope of realizing the value of our democracy and environmental protection as long as these reported regressive aliens are allowed to infiltrate power structures in a manner which conflicts with our values as forward-thinking human beings.

Introduction

On the surface, the book *Justin Trudeau, Judicial Corruption and the Supreme Court of Canada: Aliens and Archons in Our Midst* appears to focus on our current prime minister. However, this is not the case: it rather focuses on how our public perception of the apparent shortcomings of Justin Trudeau is deficient. Trying to personally lay blame on any one prime minister or government leader is therefore counterproductive.

Justin Trudeau and other leaders, whether in government or in other elite parts of society, can be more astutely regarded as mere actors or figureheads to a covert alien spectacle that is nothing short of a total violation of human sovereignty.

We as humans have Dr. Michael Salla to thank for creating a typology of a manipulative alien presence which is presented in the infographic accompanying this text. And it is this typology which also points to what might very well be the greatest conspiracy in human history: the Mandela Effect.

However, for the purposes of this book, Dr. Salla's typology would simply be an abstract concept if not for a paper trail of evil that has been associated with the oppression of Dezrin Carby-Samuels and the efforts of her son, Raymond, to liberate her from the clutches of terror and abuse perpetrated by Horace, her "husband." The apparent abuse experienced by Dezrin that was inflicted by Horace was only made worse by John Summers, a lawyer who is apparently somehow connected to an apparent underground network of judges and police, all with rather mysterious ties to the University of Ottawa.

Tracking Raymond's experiences from January 2013 into the present with his family and friends reveals a trail of the very manipulative alien interference that Dr. Salla alleges is embedded into the judicial and police control systems of society. Raymond's experience reinforces allegations which have been made not only by Dr. Salla but also by individuals testifying on YouTube that manipulative aliens have embedded themselves in society in a manner which manifests to humans as "corruption."

Raymond had been surrounded by the loving presence of family and friends up until December 31, 2012. But like so many people who have experienced the so-called Mandela Effect, just after the New Year, this began to change. Family and long-time friends began to take on different personae. Horace began to become abusive to his wife, Dezrin, who became afflicted with a mystery mental health-related illness. Rather than seeking to defend Dezrin and Raymond from abuse, family and friends simply indicated that it is "Horace's house" and he should do what he likes — which apparently included abuse. Similarly, police and a network of judges also sided with Horace the abuser under the coordination of lawyer John Summers at Bell Baker LLP in Ottawa.

Now, according to the mainstream media, the Mandela Effect is simply about masses of people having "bad memories," all of the same thing. The phenomenon got its name when Nelson Mandela passed away sometime after he had retired as president of South Africa, and it came to light that a large number of people believed Nelson Mandela had previously passed away in prison.

The popular explanation of the Mandela Effect appears to be propaganda. Rather, it seems the Mandela Effect is a result of manipulative alien-orchestrated abductions into a sophisticated artificial simulation. This apparent simulation includes characters designed to resemble our real family and friends but under the apparent control of an artificial intelligence, along with changes in our environment. When the real humans in this simulation notice these discrepancies, the apparent orchestrators of this simulation blame it on "faulty memories."

The apparent discrepancies which people have experienced between their memory and their surroundings do not seem to be the result of "forgetfulness." Rather, it has been alleged by a variety of people who have experienced the Mandela Effect that these discrepancies are the result of a discreet alien abduction scenario. In this alien abduction scenario the humans who have experienced the Mandela Effect have been moved, without our permission, into a sophisticated computer simulation of Earth.

This alleged computer simulation of Earth substantively resembles the "real Earth" but it contains discrepancies that the human abductees were not meant to notice. When the abductees become aware of these discrepancies, it results in the Mandela Effect. In this scenario, the unlikely turn of events associated with Raymond's failure to rally support among family and friends for his abused and ailing sick mother is explained by the allegation that aloof family members and friends are soulless simulations.

This "New World Order" is allegedly controlled by regressive aliens, as revealed by Dr. Salla, followed by an alleged pecking order of collaborating humans who have sold out humanity — "backdrop people," as explored in YouTube videos and clones. These "clones" might look like our real family and friends but it is apparent that they are not. Instead, according to Dr. Salla's research, it appears that these entities have been designed to be seen by us as our real family and friends while acting under a demonic alien agenda controlled by the Archons.

What has been the basis of this conclusion? Well, when these apparent clones are confronted with any information about "Old Earth," where the sun was always yellow (and not white when high up in sky like this one), and the moon appeared to us in different sizes because of this elliptical orbit (not always the same size as this "Earth"), at first their memory engrams cause them to agree and realise the discrepancy. But then all of a sudden their face goes totally blank, then they freeze, and when they wakeup out of their stupor they either say something like "Wasn't it always that way?" or sometimes react violently against the accusation that it was ever different.

My friend and others who experience life in this apparent computer simulation reminiscent of holodecs on *Star Trek* refer to this phenomenon as "downloading." In other words, the people who deny the Mandela Effect appear to be a part of this simulation and from time to time appear to be "downloading" information from a central "alien software" source to "update" these artificial life forms with the new information which differs from the original memory engrams of the humans who they resembled on the "real" or "Old Earth."

In this alien abduction scenario, people who experience the Mandela Effect have been taken away from the real Earth into a "simulated Earth" designed to manifest a "New World Order."

Corruption manifests from a lack of empathy. The corruption that we observe in the Trudeau government is simply manifestation of a system which, according to the ancient Pagan Gnostics, worships demons behind closed doors, as documented by John Lash. As the regressive alien system of control through capitalism, organized religion, and elite-driven legal systems that include law enforcement and judicial systems tightens, corruption will continue to threaten humanity's existence.

The articles related to Dezrin's plight, which are herein documented, are designed to present readers with new insights to an alleged manipulative alien orchestration through operatives embedded in human institutions.

This writer hopes that, in following the activities of Ottawa lawyer John Summers and his accomplice Marcella Carby-Samuels, working against her own mother, Dezrin Carby-Samuels, and the frustration of efforts by Raymond to liberate his mother as a result of apparent alien puppet masters which have infiltrated local police and our court system up to the Supreme Court of Canada, you will truly appreciate the dynamics of the institutionalization of corruption well beyond Trudeau's "antics."

While Dr. Salla in Infographic I documents a league of manipulative aliens which have consorted in the development of the prevailing military-industrial-political complex and global capitalist system with all its dysfuctionalities, Infographic 2 outlines documented aliens either outside or against this tyrannical complex. Dr Salla identifies the aliens in Infographic 2 as seeking to support the elevation of human consciousness away from a milieu of corruption and destructiveness against each other and our environment.

Extraterrestrial Races Cooperating with the Military-Industrial-Extraterrestrial Complex

ET Races	Main Activities	Resulting Global Problems
'Short Grays' (Zeta Reticulum & Orion)	Abducting civilians, genetic experiments, mind programming, monitoring humans through implants, cloning and creation of human-Gray hybrids.	Traumatized 'abductees', genetically modified humans humans monitored with implants mind programmed 'abductees'
'Tall Grays-Whites' (Orion)	Genetic experiments, creating a hybrid human-Gray race, mind control and diplomatic agreements with the 'shadow government'.	genetically modified humans humans monitored with implants mind programmed 'abductees' political elites compromised national security agencies infiltrated human rights abuses
Indigenous Reptilians (Earth)	Manipulating human elites, institutions & financial systems, influencing religious belief systems, militarism & removal of history of human civilization.	human rights abuses elite corruption & domination control of the media & corporations divisive religious dogma historical amnesia culture of violence
Draconian Reptilians (Alpha Draconis)	Controlling human elites, institutions & financial systems, militarism, creating a climate of scarcity, struggle and insecurity, harvesting humans, manipulating Grays and Earth Reptilians.	Concentrated global wealth & poverty Corrupt elites & institutions ethnic/religious violence, human rights abuses culture of violence & terrorism drug trade & organized crime
Sirians (Sirius B)	Participate in technology exchange programs that promote military cooperation to potential extraterrestrial threats.	Covert weapons research use of exotic weapons abuse of civilians in time travel experiments.
Anunnaki (Nibiru)	Control long term human evolution through elite groups, systems and institutions, and manipulating human consciousness. Compete with Draconians for control of Earth.	Elite manipulation religious fundamentalism patriarchal global culture culture of violence

Extraterrestrial Races Outside the Military-Industrial-Extraterrestrial Complex

ET Races	Main Activities	Assist in Global Solutions
Telosians (Earth)	Helping surface humanity learn of its ancient Earth history, restore human longevity, changing unhealthy belief systems & protecting the environment.	Environmental Protection; Promoting bio-diversity; human health & longevity; recovery of humanity's history
Lyrans (Lyra)	Disseminating the unique history of Nordic human race in the galaxy, and assisting in understanding human motivations and potentials.	recovery of humanity's history and Lyran heritage; understanding galactic history; discovery of the human essence; diplomacy & conflict resolution; global education
Vegans (Lyra)	Disseminating the unique history of the darker/blue skinned human race in the galaxy, and assisting in understanding human motivations and potentials.	recovery of humanity's history and Vegan heritage; understanding galactic history; discovery of the human essence; diplomacy & conflict resolution; global education
Pleiadians (Pleiades)	find freedom from oppressive structures through consciousness raising	universal human rights; participatory democratic systems; evolution of human consciousness; global education
Procyons (Procyon)	Promoting effective resistance to extraterrestrial subversion, developing 'multidimensional consciousness', using mental imagery to prevent ET mind control, monitoring unfriendly ET activity	Exposing ET subversion; ending global secrecy of ETs; multidimensional consciousness; deprogramming mind control; universal human rights; internet & global communication
Tau Cetians (Tau Ceti)	Exposing ET subversion & control, identifying corrupt elites & institutions, uplifting human consciousness, negating ET mind control and dealing with militarism.	exposing government/ financial corruption & elite manipulation; monitoring ET infiltration; multidimensional consciousness; deprogramming mind control; conflict resolution
Andromedans (Andromeda)	Facilitating decisions of the Galactic community in dealing with the current Earth situation, innovative strategies for resolving conflict, the education of youth, and crop circles	education of psychic/crystal kids; peace education; exposing elite manipulation; improved global governance; diplomacy & conflict resolution; extraterrestrial communications
Sirians (Sirius A)	Assisting in building a suitable ecological system for (human) evolution on Earth by altering the 'bio-magnetic energy grid' of the planet.	Environmental Protection; Promoting bio-diversity; raising human consciousness; evolution of the biosphere
Ummites (Ummo)	Sharing technical information, transforming scientific culture, and global education.	Transforming scientific paradigms; Developing alternative technologies; Educational reform
Alpha Centaurians (Alpha Centauri)	Promoting social justice and human freedom, and responsible use of advanced technology.	Social justice at a global level; zones of peace; human rights; sustainable development
Arcturians (Arcturus)	Integrating spiritual values with advanced technologies, in providing strategic advice in transforming planetary systems, and crop circles.	global governance; integrating global financial, political and societal systems; coordinating relationships with ETs; diplomacy and conflict resolution; extraterrestrial communications

Infographics adopted with permission courtesy of Dr. Michael Salla from "A Report on the Motivations and Activities of Extraterrestrial Races – A Typology of the Most Significant Extraterrestrial Races Interacting with Humanity" in Exopolitics: Report on the Political Implications of the Extraterrestrial Presence, Revised January 1, 2005 (First published July 26, 2004).

The Mandela Effect: A New World Order Experiment — Humans, Artificial Life Forms and Orchestrated Events?

I often used to hear the term "New World Order" and simply regarded it as a synonym for "corporate globalization." However, it has become apparent to me that it may be so much more.

Back in 2016, I first heard the term "Mandela Effect." At that time, it was explained to me as referring to the phenomenon of groups of people recalling that Nelson Mandela had passed away in prison, in contrast with an official timeline that stated Nelson Mandela had died many years after he was released from prison and after he served as president of South Africa. My roommate at the time told me about how more and more people were beginning to remember things differently than what has been shown to be the official version of things. This phenomenon has been well-discussed in Facebook groups, and many of these discussions revolve around the idea that people were being pushed into an "alternative reality" in which popular culture and brand-name icons were different than what they remember.

I too recall a "timeline" of Nelson Mandela having passed away in prison and then seemingly "magically" being freed from prison and eventually becoming South African president. But at the time I simply shrugged it off as some sort of oddity not worth thinking about. However, mass media pundits, when referring to the so-called Mandela Effect, will simply describe it as somehow "proving" that humans have "bad memories" that cause them to remember things wrong. Oh, really? How are all these humans all having such distinct and clear memories of certain things? Is this phenomenon the result of a collective "group or mass senility" regarding the memory of such things as the Statute of Liberty being on Ellis Island and not Liberty Island, as it is currently, along with people's memory of a smaller and always yellow sun in our sky instead of the sometimes white and much larger sun we see today? What about other changes to the world map which have been documented by many Mandela Effect experiencers? For example, how is South America all-of-a-sudden now so much closer to Africa than it once was, and what accounts for Cuba becoming bigger, New Zealand changing positions, or other apparent geographic modifications in the current world map? I'm a geographer who has been drawing maps of the world from my head since Grade 1 and there has most definitely been some kind of space-time distortion.

Now, you may at this stage wonder what all this has to do with Justin Trudeau, Dezrin Carby-Samuels, and the macabre sequence of events outlined in this book. Well, I've come to understand that the Mandela Effect is much more than it appeared to be at first glance. It can be described as a mass alien abduction event scenario associated with relatively small populations of humans having been abducted into a very sophisticated artificial simulation in which humans who experience the Mandela Effect are being forced to interact with artificial replicas of relatives and friends. People who experience the Mandela Effect often report shocking experiences in which loved ones look the same but act in totally different ways, resulting in their having become estranged from one another.

I have even seen cases of the so-called Mandela Effect in which humans have been kicked out of their homes by apparent artificial life forms. People who experience the Mandela Effect report that when they have sought to confront such relatives and friends with firm historical events they have always known to be accurate, the relatives and friends would at first agree with them, but would then inextricably freeze, their eyes would glaze over, and then they would adamantly deny what they had only moments before agreed to as fact. Humans who have experienced this phenomenon report that it appears as if these "people" were receiving a "download," like some kind of android. The "people" who receive these apparent downloads have been described as "backdrop people." These backdrop people have been described as cloned replicas with memories of the real humans they are made to resemble but whose minds are being operated from a centralized source which enables them to receive "downloads." These apparent downloads are designed to correct any information which originates from the "Old Earth," where their consciousness had originated.

It is apparent that the so-called Mandela Effect has manifested in a bizarre sequencing of historical events like the election of Justin Trudeau in spite of the fact that just before the election that made him prime minister he had been the leader of a third-place party behind both the Stephen Harper Conservatives and the NDP led by Thomas Mulcair. But more significantly for this book, regarding the estrangement of family members, it is clear that events surrounding the oppression of Dezrin Carby-Samuels and the apparently futile efforts of her son to rescue her seem to be an artificially orchestrated scenario of the demonic architects of the Mandela Effect and the backdrop people that collaborate with them.

By reading this book, you will be looking through a window into scenarios carefully orchestrated and designed by the demonic architects to somehow feed off the negative energy created by Dezrin's son's experiences of frustration in his efforts to liberate his mother from abuse by her husband and the lawyer appointed to perpetuate this frustration.

This book is designed to show how what we may often describe as corruption may simply be orchestrations by aliens aimed at enforcing control while feeding-off of our negative energy. As we become increasingly frustrated in an environment where artificial life forms that appear as people are part of a physical environment which resembles the real Earth but is not the same, we create more negative energy. But as we humans begin to wake-up, we are beginning to notice more and more how we have somehow been the subject of alien-directed collusion, a theory presented by Dr. Michael Salla. The Mandela Effect can therefore be described not as showing how "forgetful" we are as humans but rather as an awakening to an alien abduction for the minority of the population who are real humans and not the apparent soulless replicas that dominate the population of this new world — this New Earth.

One YouTube researcher suggests that humans have been abducted from what he describes as a "Free Earth" in the Sagittarius belt of the Milky Way galaxy and taken into what he describes as a "Controlled Earth," which he maps as being in the Orion belt. It therefore may not be a coincidence that one of the demonic alien groups in the infographic designed from Dr. Michael Salla's typology of demonic aliens has been described by John Lash and other researchers as having the technology capacity to manifest artificial life and simulations designed to manipulate humanity as residing the Orion system. Are the abducted humans who now experience the Mandela Effect experiencing a sort of New World Order controlled by artificial life forms which feed off of the frustration experienced by human populations that have been abducted from Old Earth?

Marginalization: A legal system which doesn't respect the spirit of Canada's Charter of Rights and Freedoms

arginalized groups which our *Canadian Charter of Rights and Free-doms* seeks to support are being needlessly perpetuated by an archaic and regressive legal system. The Charter's promise in its 1982 constitutional enactment of a forward-thinking egalitarian, cosmopolitan community and 'Just Society' is being held back. A neo-colonial system of law which was well entrenched in Canadian society from the nineteenth century has promoted an elite structure of power which actively seeks to frustrate marginalized Canadians through judges who prevail over the justice system; lawyers; and the police. It has become self-evident that many judges, lawyers and the police in their behavioural norms view the Charter as a threat to their "authority". This authority has brought with it both economic and political power in association with maintaining corporate power, which is largely under the patriarchal control of wealthy white males. It is apparent that affluent white males whose wealth has been accrued from legal infringements like those which stole the lands of First Nations and have denied women opportunities have sought to maintain legally oppressive control through an organized "Fifth Column" of judges, lawyers, and police who preside over a culture of law inimical to Charter rights. In order for the "Charter's promise" for a rejuvenated context of "equal rights for all" among rights and freedoms to be fulfilled, Canada's entire legal system must be rejuvenated to promote empathy and accessibility for all regardless of economic or other status.

In order for our legal system and its outcomes through litigation and other means to reflect the Charter's values, the system must begin to fully embrace accessibility. Through Section 24(1) of the Charter, Canadians are empowered with having the right to affirm their rights and freedoms through courts of law. But individuals from marginalized communities cannot effectively seek to "de-marginalize" themselves when police, lawyers, and judges operate within a culture in which the active pursuit of justice is reserved for those who have the wealth to hire the expensive lawyers needed to interpret laws and to navigate a legal system the average Canadian can barely, if at all, comprehend.

The *Canada Health Act*, inspired by Tommy Douglas, who sought to "de-marginalize" Canadians in matters of healthcare, provides a constructive basis to progressively move our legal system to "de-marginalize" Canadians from legal oppression. Through a *Canada Health Act*-inspired context, Canadians who face ongoing infringements to their Charter rights would be able to access universal legal assistance in a way that corresponds to the manner by which Canadians currently obtain medical assistance. Once Canadians have been empowered through universal access to lawyers, who are in turn sensitized to the vital importance of serving all Canadians in a manner which promotes equality and justice for all, the lawyers promoted to positions as judges will have been socialized to embrace a progressive system of constitutional governance, which will help to transform policing. A new culture of lawyers who embrace universality would help to support a rejuvenated legal culture in replacing the current neo-colonial system of patriarchal laws with a legal system based in the same down-to-earth language that inspired the writing of our Charter toward a de-marginalized society

─────·≫≡≡≡≡≪·─────

The Fifth Column: The Secret War against the Canadian Charter of Rights and Freedoms

Our *Canadian Charter of Rights and Freedoms* has truly become a substantive reflection of the legal ideals held by a broadening majority of Canadians. This observation is based upon statistical data from national firms that claim to have a very small margin of error. It would therefore perhaps be considered unfortunate by this broadening majority that the *Canadian Charter of Rights and Freedoms'* apparent promise of an egalitarian society in matters of civil rights appears to be stifled by a perpetuating context of marginalization. Indeed, it appears that marginalization is increasingly becoming a fact of life for many Canadians despite the equalizing effect that the Charter is supposed to have.

The aim of this book is part is to help illuminate the apparent presence of a system of organized socio-legal thought that reinforces oppressive patriarchal norms in our society, which manifests in marginalization. This system of socio-legal thought ossifies and stifles Canada's entire system and the administration of justice in a manner which is incongruent with the Charter's intent of creating the "Just Society" envisioned by former Prime Minister Pierre Elliot Trudeau.

When Canadians picture a judge in our Canadian system of justice, they likely envision a highly noble character like Frank Iacobucci, CC QC, who was a *puisne justice* of the Supreme Court of Canada from 1991 to 2004 when he retired from the bench, and a staunch defender of human rights and supporter of the Charter. However, we would be forgetting our colonial past, which produced a system of law and administration of justice founded in that colonial past, with actors who preside over that system and seek to maintain it. It is this system and culture which is responsible for marginalization.

There are two discernible schools of legal thought, which creates confusion between the way in which the system is supposed to operate and the way the system appears to operate most of the time. The school of legal thought that inspired the creation of the Charter could be best described as "egalitarianism," which regards equity as a central basis to guide desirable legal outcomes in relation to the operation of justice. However, the second and perhaps most dominant school of legal thought is held by what can be best referred to as the "apologists";it is this school of thought which Leo Strauss sought to convey and galvanize through his books, teachings and movement.

This book will therefore seek to inspire an exploration of the apparent intellectual prism which shapes the enforcement of oppression and marginalization. The three principle actors of this system are judges, lawyers and the police. The apologists' intellectual prism shapes these actors' apparent worldview, which was articulated by Leo Strauss, who wrote books in law and philosophy. Former U.S. Supreme Court Justice Clarence Thomas was one of Leo Strauss's former students. However, Leo Strauss's socio-legal thought permeates the thinking of principal actors in The Establishment in general, and in the legal system specifically, who seek to resist values which they view as being threatened by legal values of equity and social justice.

Both the egalitarians and the apologists believe in the idea of democracy, but their views on the roles of law and democracy are in opposition to one another. Egalitarians who are inspired by the Charter embrace the diversity and pluralism of Canada and look to the Charter as a constitutional mechanism for supporting inclusion and fulfilling governance in a participatory democracy. In contrast, the apologists embrace what they view to be the proper original construct of democracy in early Greece, which limited the exercise of governance to the most wise, learned and wealthy men of society. In the apologist view, "elites" have an inherent "natural right" to exercise authority. Apologists championed by Leo Strauss and Murray Rothbard despised the "liberal" idea of democracy as a dangerous idea which would create a tyranny run by unruly masses.

In 1935, having written the book *Philosophy and Law: Contributions to the Understanding of Maimonides and His Predecessors***, Leo Strauss went onto write in** *Liberalism Ancient and Modern* **(1968), in which he says:**

> It was once said that democracy is the regime that stands or falls by virtue: a democracy is a regime in which all or most adults are men of virtue, and since virtue seems to require wisdom, a regime in which all or most adults are virtuous and wise, or the society in which all or most adults have developed their reason to a high degree, or the rational society. **Democracy, in a word, is meant to be an aristocracy which has broadened into a universal aristocracy.** … There exists a whole science—the science which I among thousands of others profess to teach… —which so to speak has no other theme than the contrast between the original conception of democracy, or what one may call the ideal of democracy, and democracy as it is. (pp. 4–5)

The apologists don't regard the Charter as "substantive law" which should inherently moderate their exercise of power. Rather, apologists view the Charter to be a myth that is useful for pacifying the masses so that they feel good about themselves while the exercise of patriarchal legal power continues to operate on behalf of the natural rights of its rules, as it always has. In *Natural Right and History* (1953) Leo Strauss further characterizes marginalization as natural; he claims that people of relative superiority naturally form the upper strata of society that those people who are marginalized are in such a position as a result of having inferior qualities that relegate them to a lower strata, and that the legal system should not interfere with such societal differentiation.

> The character, or tone, of a society depends on what the society regards as the most respectable or most worthy of admiration. But by regarding certain habits or attitudes as most respectable, a society ad-

mits the superiority, the superior dignity, of those human beings who most perfectly embody the habits or attitudes in question. That is to say, every society regards a specific human type (or a specific mixture of human types) as authoritative. When the authoritative type is the common man, everything has to justify itself before the tribunal of the common man; everything which cannot be justified before that tribunal becomes, at best, merely tolerated, if not despised or suspect. And even those who do not recognize that tribunal are, willy-nilly, moulded by its verdicts. (p. 137)

In rejecting the Charter, the silent rallying cry of the apologist thought which dominates legal governance in Canada is the old British North American Act phrase "Peace, Order and Good Government."

The legal theorizing of Murray Rothbard is evident in the manner in which the prevailing actors in our legal system seem to have such a hypocritical and lethargic response when dealing with inequity and injustice in relation to the Charter's desire to advance equality. In Rothbard's book *Egalitarianism as a Revolt Against Nature* (1974), he elaborates that "almost everyone assumes that equality is a 'good thing'." Rothbard goes on to pose the question, "Why assume that equality is desirable?"

Rothbard argues in support of a "correct ethics" in accord with nature, which ought to pivot on the "survival of the fittest," and that efforts to affirm "equality" as central to justice, as the Charter seeks to support, are inherently "un-natural" and would only lead to "tyranny" by "undisciplined masses" who lack the wisdom and overall superiority of the upper strata. Leo Strauss echoed this theme in his book *On Tyranny* (1963), which further provides a socio-legal analytical framework for understanding the apparent organized perpetuation of conditions for marginalization alongside legal inequity. The apologists out of the media spotlight would further argue, as Leo Strauss had, that the creation of myths is a useful device to unify the masses under the control of its rulers who preside over the legal system and, as a result, the "modus operandi" of the legal system should not be bound by the Charter as it is by and large a useful instrument of propaganda.

Rothbard broadens his criticisms of equality in *Freedom, Inequality, Primitivism and the Division of Labor* (1970). In this further expansion of the apologist plane of socio-legal consciousness, he asserts that not only do biology and history make human beings inherently different from one another, but that civilization depends on these differences. To the apologist, marginalization should not be eradicated under the "equality rubric" of the Charter's "public myth making," but rather, should be embraced as part of "the natural order of things" in a "Great Society." The marginalization of First Nations and individuals in "so-called" oppressed communities are simply the outcomes of "God's Will" that manifests in human civilization. In America, such an embracing of "God's Will" is expressed in that nation's national motto, "In God We Trust," and such a belief is similarly vaunted in Canada.

Today in Canadian society, the apparent legal enforcement of marginalization has empowered the ability of the "haves" to oppress and worsen the conditions of the "have nots" against the spirit of the Charter. When Canadians believe their protected rights and freedoms are being infringed, they are supposed to able to rely on re-asserting those rights through Section 24(1) of the *Canadian Charter of Rights and Freedoms.* This section empowers all Canadians to be able to apply to a court of competent jurisdiction to obtain the protection of those rights and freedoms, which the court is supposed to defend without prejudice.

Indeed, our Charter is only as strong as the extent to which Canadians can easily enforce their rights free of systemic barriers. However, the author has studied the inner workings of the Ontario court system for more than three years, and finds it apparent that marginalized Canadians face three distinct barriers that have been designed to prevent "have nots," or more specifically, legally disenfranchised individuals, from challenging the elites who hold positions as the lawyers and judges that preside over the justice system in general and specifically the administration of justice.

Barrier number one is that the lawyers who preside over the system have created a culture that demands financial compensation, which limits the use of lawyers to the most financially affluent Canadians. Barrier number two is that the system dissuades the average Canadian from being able to easily represent themselves in court without a lawyer by creating a system of language and formality including court procedures which elude the comprehension of most Canadians. However, the third barrier, which is unknown to most Canadians because of the difficulty marginalized Canadians have in successfully getting around barriers number one and two is that judges in the Canadian system who cling to a Straussian socio-legal view will be predisposed to totally ignore a challenge by a marginalized Canadian to the legal Establishment, irrespective of any evidence or soundness of presentation which that Canadian may present.

It is this third barrier, which has shown itself in cases of racism, sexism, and other discriminations that have subverted the equitable rendering of judicial decisions, which reveals a Straussian prism behind a perpetuated context of marginalization faced by First Nations, visible minorities, women, homeless, the working poor, the sick, the disabled, many seniors, and other disenfranchised Canadians.

The Canadian court system presents a context in which judges who would be inclined to defend Charter rights in the spirit of Supreme Court Justice Frank Iacobucci, when out of the spotlight of a case that has garnered mass media attention, face pressure from the patriarchal system to thwart any challenge brought to it by a self-represented marginalized Canadian who has managed to evade the "natural barriers" of lack of financial wherewithal and a legal education on the court system which have been designed to keep marginalized Canadians "in their place".

The judges are appointed from lawyers, who, in turn, are from a profession known for often supporting and helping to prosecute in favour of the property and other interests of the most wealthy Canadians against marginalized individuals who have been disenfranchised by the prevailing legal system, and the police are the "front lines" of the perpetuation of marginalization on behalf of the Establishment. Together, through a "Straussian" prism and neo-colonial system and administration of justice, these actors work as a "fifth column" against the ability of Canadians to constructively use the Charter to "de-marginalize" themselves.

Arguably, the Charter is an insufficient constitutional enactment to empower all Canadians who seek to defend their rights and freedoms from infringements. For the Charter to be able to "do its job," the prevailing Canadian legal system and administration of justice would firstly need to affirm universal access to lawyers in a regulated system analogous to the Canada Health Act, which supports universal access by Canadians to doctors and healthcare. Secondly, even if Canadians are empowered with universal access to lawyers, it would be vital for the entire system of laws to be rewritten in a manner inspired by the down-to-earth language of the Charter and the formality of the court system and police authority to reflect that of public service to all Canadians based upon the values of the Charter and not based on the context of patriarchy which presently dominates our legal system.

The apologists would argue away from the media spotlight that the central role of the justice system is not to support equitable outcomes like those also envisioned by Section 96 of the *Ontario Courts of Justice Act*. Rather, the apologists would argue that the central role of justice is simply to defend "the system" and that "equality" ought to be regarded as no more than an accidental by-product of the system, which may have been simply created to provide a theatrical illusion that the system supports equality.

Some may consider the apologist school of socio-legal thought to be cynical. But the apologists would regard themselves as true "realists" who appreciate the role of law in a capitalist system such as Canada's, and recognize marginalization as a necessary part of the system—after all, for society to work, not everyone can be equally legally empowered.

The role of law in the "realist" and also "pragmatic" thinking of the apologists is therefore to view actors who prevail over the legal system as entrusted "managers" of "natural inequities" who are there to maintain "Peace, Order and Good Government," as expressed in the former *British North America Act, 1867*. The role of the prevailing actors of the legal system in apologist thinking is not to push our system to the brink of a "tyranny of the masses" by an unending march to equity, but rather to promote equitable outcomes in selected court decisions and other legal matters that can be used to promote the "myth of equality."

While the Charter envisions judges as impartial purveyors of the system, by acknowledging the existence of the apologists, the author furthermore proposes to present a rejuvenated perspective of judges as "astute political actors." In the spotlight of high-profile cases such as gay marriage, which has garnered sufficient media attention and public support, judges would be wise to support these rights in order to legitimate the court as standing up for legal equity and affirming the values of the Charter. However, these same judges, outside the media spotlight, are free to engage in ignoring any litigant who, in coming from a marginalized community, is without the money to pay the price demanded by lawyers in the commodification of civil rights that apologists seek to maintain.

Thus, while egalitarians envision judges as the impartial purveyors of the system supported by the *Canadian Charter of Rights and Freedoms*, the apologists view judges as being astute political actors who decide on cases in matters of equality based upon how much media attention there may be in any particular case they preside over.

Alien elites seek to bring together worlds

What intelligence whistleblowers like Edward Snowden and others have revealed about the scale of human surveillance worldwide was not a revelation to me. Research these subjects at any length and to any depth and you will know that there are two worlds, the seen and the unseen, operating in the same 'space' while masquerading as one.

First there is the world that humanity in general experiences as the 'seen'. This is where governments are chosen by the ballot box through something called 'democracy' and from this come laws and regulations that apply to everyone, including governments, intelligence agencies, law enforcement, military, and so on. This world doesn't really exist in any form except in theory and the structure of government and 'democracy' in all its expressions is there to control the population, not to hold itself to account. The 'laws' apply only to the 'little people', with increasingly rare exceptions, while the other world does as it likes.

It is the realm of Satanism, secret societies, semi-secret groups, banks and corporations that dictate public policy and the direction of human society by imposing the laws from the shadows which, in the world of the seen, appear on the surface to be the work of politicians accountable to The People through open debate and elections.

In this realm of the unseen there are no laws or checks and balances on unfettered power. It is, after all, the realm created by unfettered power to infinitely expand unfettered power. In short, it does whatever it wants without challenge or accountability, except in the sense that lower levels of the unseen are strictly accountable to those above them.

The unseen hierarchy is accountable only to itself and not at all to the hierarchy of the seen that we see as governments, intelligence agencies, law enforcement and military. Once you realise this there is nothing in theme that even an insider like Edward Snowden can tell you that is not already obvious, a gimme.

The fact that so many – not least in the media – have reacted with shock and outrage shows just how firewalled the unseen is from the perceptions of the seen. I share the outrage, but not the shock.

CHAPTER 1

JUSTIN TRUDEAU – Simply a window to corruption

The Raybould Affair - Justin Trudeau Presides Over Cesspool of Corruption, Sexism, and Racism

Having worked for Ministers in the federal government, let's start dealing with reality on "The Raybould Affair".

The truth of the matter is that Canada doesn't have an independent judiciary that's substantively inspired by the ideals of our Canadian Constitution. Indeed, this is what I have documented in my coming book.

Our Canadian Judicial system is essentially corrupt and Jody Wilson-Raybould's selfless act to stand-up against it has exposed just how rotten it is.

When Justin Trudeau recently asserted that "diversity only works if there's trust" what he meant to say is that women and visible minorities are only welcomed in our Canadian system of government if they are seen and not heard and turn a blind eye to their ethical responsibilities to integrity. And, if they are asked by the white male-dominated system to do certain things which are essentially corrupt then that is their job to execute; and if they ever dare inform the public of the corrupt ways of the system, then they deserved to be kicked to the curb and humiliated. That's the core belief system that has perpetuated unspeakable social injustices in Canada.

When I had worked in government, I was offered a fabulous job with the Canadian Human Rights Commission.

However, they demanded that every time a file is brought before me for investigation, they would require me to automatically dismiss any applicant's file for a human rights investigation as being without merit.

That's when I decided that my soul was not for sale, and I took myself out of the cesspool of government.

Justin Trudeau's reported efforts to interfere in the work and the Office of the Minister of Justice, is a typical way of doing business not just in Ottawa but across government in Canada.

Raybould's apparent miscalculation in my view is that she may have been watching too much American TV and forgot that she was in Canada which still operates substantively based upon colonial norms.

If she was in the United States, her actions would have gotten a lot more public support and she probably would have been able to weather the storm in the Cabinet and champion reforms.

However, because of how our political system is set up, which fuses the power in the Office of the Prime Minister, Raybould didn't have much of a chance.

Jody Wilson-Raybould's case shows that politics in Canada these days is no place for anyone who has a smack of integrity.

Our whole system is dominated by corrupt lawyers who either become corrupt politicians doing "their thing" like Justin Trudeau or instead become corrupt judges and the most corrupt of them get promoted by the corrupt ex-lawyer politicians to Canada's Supreme Court. Indeed, our so-called 'Supreme Court' remains a bastion of Canada's corrupt, racist and neo-colonial norms - not a black, Asian, South Asian or other such visible minorities in the "High Court".

As an investigative journalist, I can tell you that the idea of "judicial independence" in Canada is a complete myth and farce.

Judges in Canada are substantively influenced by who has power and who doesn't in and out of the courtroom. If you're a self-represented litigant who hasn't received any attention by the mass media, it is likely they won't even bother taking even one minute to examine your case that's opposed by one of their lawyer colleagues.

Judges in Canada regularly consult with various elites who then direct these judges who to support and reject the substantive operation of Kangaroo Courts in Canada. So when Justin Trudeau reportedly asked Raybould to do certain things for his "friends" in the Montreal "Château Clique" that was not Mr. Trudeau being corrupt on his own. Rather, that sort of sought favour by Mr. Trudeau was a normal way of doing business among the lawyers of our system who act as judges or as politicians.

Raybould's role in all of this was not only to help maintain the charade, but also to facilitate it by responding to Trudeau's desires, and not stand up against it.

Raybould seems to have thought that she could challenge the corrupt norms that operate behind closed doors on a day-to-day basis and Justin Trudeau has made it known just how wrong she is.

As Maclean's recently proclaimed, Justin is an "imposter". His Sunny Ways" that he sought to extol when he took office was a sham and a scam,

Thanks to former Minister Raybould for showing us just a glimpse of just how corrupt our system has become under the Archons who sell out our Canadian Dream to fascistic and self-serving egos.

Raybould's big mistake was that she truly believed in the official propaganda taught in Canadian political science classrooms that the Minister of Justice's role is to champion the rule of law and the integrity of our system of justice from political interference. Ms. Raybould was too much of a romantic idealist for her former job.

Like Ministers of Justice before, she should have realized when she took the job that Mr. Trudeau simply wanted her to "decorate" his Cabinet as both a female and First Nations face to legitimate his hypocrisy that he actually gives a damn about women and other visible minorities while also "doing what she's told to do" behind closed doors along with the other representatives of the judicial system right down to judges across this land who prostitute themselves of elite political manipulation.

I give a toast to Madame Raybould for showing us just a glimpse of the morbid corruption of not only this Justin Trudeau government, but other governments across Canada, which usually operate in the dark hall of boardrooms under the auspices of the elite-driven political-military-industrial complex. This complex is maintained by corrupt lawyers with the various hats of power that they wear to maintain power in this country which is bereft of principles of equity and values of democracy.

CHAPTER 2

ARCHONS – Beyond Justin Trudeau

Scheer Evil: Tory Loyalist Criticizes The Conservative Party's Hidden Agenda

My fellow Canadians, you may have heard a phrase which asserts that those of us who refuse to learn the lessons of history are condemned to repeat it.

So let's not worsen the damage that our country has sustained with the even greater wrecking ball which Andrew Scheer's so-called Conservative Party represents.

The worst-kept secret of Andrew Scheer's Conservative Party in this federal election is its hidden agenda: a plot to continue the work of the former Stephen Harper government through "change agents."

This demonic tactic was used by the former Stephen Harper government to inject operatives, who would intentionally sabotage the workings of public service in a manner designed to create public outcry.

Having succeeded in this mission, Harper's Archontic "political apparatchiks" would then seek to present the idea of privatization to the Canadian public in order to enable the sale of government assets to right-wing interests that helped to finance or otherwise support the election of the Conservative Party.

There is nothing new about this hidden agenda of Andrew Scheer's entourage. Wiki characterizes this ploy as the "Problem Reaction Solution" (Latin: *ordo ab chao*),referring to it as a "mass mind control system. It is used to make changes to the law that the citizens would not accept otherwise."

The practitioners of this strategy are not Conservatives at all in the Canadian sense, or in any sense, for that matter. Rather, this is an approach used by the far-right Neo-Fascists that parachuted themselves from Preston Manning's former Reform Party into the then Progressive Conservative party and ever since have sought to conceal their globalist Nazi aspirations with the adoption of the Conservative label.

The hidden agenda of Andrew Scheer's Neo-Fascists includes the following six reported approaches designed to destroy the vitality of our public service in support of all Canadians.

First, Scheer intends to hire "fifth columns" as directors and senior managers across the public services. In a position of power, these individuals would instruct employees to "let things go" at all levels.

Secondly, he aims to target public servants who ignore these directives and work passionately at their jobs through gaslighting.

Gaslighting is a form of psychological manipulation in which a person seeks to sow seeds of doubt in a targeted individual or in members of a targeted group, making them question their own memory, perception, and sanity. Using persistent denial, misdirection, contradiction, and lying, gaslighting involves attempts to destabilize the victim and delegitimize the victim's beliefs.

I can tell you that this is 100 percent true because I personally witnessed these change agents cajole, demoralize, and harass my father until he literally became crazy. As a result of this gaslighting he is now a shadow of the man he once was.

The third part of Andrew Scheer's Neo-Fascist playbook designed to continue Stephen Harper's unfinished work is to then intentionally hire easily controllable and incompetent people in government to manipulate the Canadian public to further demand privatization; the Neo-Fascists, aka the Conservatives, would then offer it as "the solution."

This is not to say that Justin Trudeau has not adopted some of these strategies in certain areas of government, like parts of our public healthcare system, or in dealing with responsibilities with First Nations. However, the present impact of change agents under the current Trudeau government would most definitely worsen exponentially under the backroom demonic puppet-masters orchestrating Andrew Scheer's campaign.

The fourth strategy Sheer will adopt, which was employed by the Harper government, is to further psychologically terrorize government employees by letting them know they are being watched by a network of informants to ensure that they carry out their orders to "let things go." When public servants cannot be easily fired for ignoring these orders, they will be subjected to malicious gaslighting tactics designed to induce mental illness and an inability to work, or to drive them to seek early retirement or buyout, to use public service jargon.

The fifth strategy which supporters of an Andrew Scheer government would seek in fulfillment of ex-prime minister Stephen Harper's stratagem is to further break down the integrity of our public service through a strategy of "divide, rule or conquer." In this strategy, so-called change agents are used to mischievously instigate quarrels and rifts in the office to create an environment that is as psychologically oppressive as possible, with the goal of bringing work to a halt.

The sixth strategy is to intentionally move personnel into new jobs without any training, and then for managerial change agents to psychologically terrorize the moved employees to achieve impossible job performance targets. When these targets are not achieved, the Conservative Party change agents would be instructed to humiliate the moved employees in front of their peers and then write humiliating performance appraisals.

Again, the goal of this strategy is to demoralize competent employees so that they lose their mind and voluntarily leave government. Many tens of thousands of extremely professional and experienced public servants have departed government as a result of such tactics.

Conservative Party tactics also exploit racism and sexism. The Conservative Party playbook seems to target both visible minorities and women as the most vulnerable to a system of change agent tactics. Conservative Party change agents would seek to exploit racial and other prejudices harboured in the workplace to further employ tactics of psychological terrorism and warfare against the vitality of our Canadian public service in support of vital social and other services that we, as Canadians, rely on in our everyday lives.

The system of informants used to observe and enforce these six strategies of the so-called change agents is right out of the old playbook of Communist East Germany and other former Soviet Eastern Bloc countries which created an environment of widespread fear that one's neighbours or even one's own spouse could be a government informant.

Indeed, it is hardly surprising that Stephen Harper and his clique would be architects of such a ploy, which manifests from his alleged support of the Nazi-inspired ideology of Leo Strauss.

As a Canadian Tory, I implore all Canadians to vote "Anything But Scheer" if you value a strong public service composed of competent people who take pride in the work they do for Canadians and who value your trust as a Canadian taxpayer.

Make no mistake — Andrew Scheer and the background entourage which now seeks to re-seize control of Canada to finish the work of Stephen Harper are in no way the real Canadian Conservatives who, as Tories, sought to advocate for many of the values that we now identify as Canadian.

We Canadian Tories had originally sought to champion our Confederation in 1867 under the election of Prime Minister Sir John A. Macdonald that was based upon values which viewed a strong federal government as vital to our national interests. We can thank our commitment to a strong federal government for the blossoming of our modern bilingual and multicultural Canada.

Through the hidden agenda of change agents, today's so-called Conservative Party under leader Andrew Scheer seeks to destroy Canada and allow its public assets to be consumed by billionaire foreign nationals in the United States, China, Europe and elsewhere. If you value a strong Canada, improvements to public healthcare and the protection of our environment in support of the health of voters and their families, then the only way to go in this federal election is "Anything But Scheer." Let's turn away from the impostor Conservative Party, which presents no change in the direction which values a strong public service that works hard for all Canadians.

Andrew Scheer makes no apologies for his close ideological association with Stephen Harper, who is an official founder of an extreme right-wing group that championed the former racist pro-Apartheid South African government which kept Nelson Mandela in prison for decades.

This group, The Northern Foundation, was revealed by Project Democracy in 2013.

In light of this history, it is no wonder that Andrew Scheer made such a relatively lacklustre challenge to Justin Trudeau's "blackface" and "brownface" revelations as compared to NDP Jagmeet Singh and other Canadian political voices.

Racism is one apparent pillar of The Northern Foundation. The other apparent pillar is the very breakdown and break-up of government through insidious "fifth columns."

The Reform Party had been an apparent political incarnation of The Northern Foundation. Later, the Reform Party essentially took-over the Conservative Party.

As Project Democracy documents:

"The Northern Foundation was established in 1989, originally as a pro-South Africa [and an aggressive champion of Apartheid] group. It lists among the founding members both William Gairdner and Stephen Harper. The Northern Foundation was the creation of a number of generally extreme right-wing conservatives, including Anne Hartmann (a director of REAL Women), Geoffrey Wasteneys (a long-standing member of the Alliance for the Preservation of English in Canada), George Potter (also a member of the Alliance), author Peter Brimelow, Link Byfield (son of Ted Byfield and publisher/president of Alberta Report), and Stephen Harper. [Harper] was then considered to be from the 'extreme right-wing.'"

A vote for Andrew Scheer's Conservative Party is therefore a vote not for Conservatism as it existed through statesmen like Sir John A. Macdonald, John Diefenbaker, Robert Stanfield and former Ontario premier Bill Davis, but instead a vote for a neo-fascist entity which seeks to destroy our entire system of public and social services on behalf of an oppressive private corporate mafia. Scheer's essential fascist agenda is apparent in the extreme centralized control his party exerts over his own candidates, which is a mockery of democracy.

A Scheer government promises not only to expedite the entire breakdown of our system of public and social services through change agents, but to then breakup all our public and other national assets and distribute them into the hands of major private campaign contributors who are affiliated with large transnational interests. In this idealized form of government, our House of Commons would be essentially replaced by government under the direction of a "politburo" similar to the Chinese Communist one-party state and heads of corporations, and who are all members of the one-party state under Andrew Scheer and his cronies of a political-military-industrial-complex.

Global Crisis: Aliens rule humanity through Archons

The scientific community pretty much agrees that the human race evolved in the Great Rift Valley of East Africa around 200,000 years ago. Wherever it may have been, the Garden of Eden was not in Africa. So where does that leave Adam and Eve? One recent theory is that Adam and Eve and their descendants are alien contrived entities. Did Adam and Eve come in our human space-time (possible from the moon) to populate it with their kind, and to take the best resources of this planet (notably gold)? Once established, did the descendants of the Adam and Eve bloodline, as David Sewell War and David Icke suggest, conspire to manipulate Earth?

Alex Collier thinks that there are two kinds of aliens – Ethical ones and Manipulative ones. He claims to be in constant contact with Ethical Human Extraterrestrials who keep him informed about happenings and conflicts among entities in distant galaxies. With the insights that his contacts have provided to him, Collier has concluded that much of what we believe is the product of the infiltration by lower-dimensional aliens of artificial intelligence that we, as humans, have allowed into our collective human consciousness.

Apparently, lower-dimensional aliens seek to exploit negative energies that humans can generate. Archons, based on Dr. John Lash's insights are not "Extraterrestrials" from distant planets, but, instead, are entities from a parallel reality. Such entities seek to live out their ego-driven and artificial intelligence-directed lives at the expense of humans who are higher dimensional spiritual biological begins.

Collier is convinced that lower-dimensional "Archons" invaded the Earth in the 1930s (some believe at the invitation of the Nazi's) and that both the Creationist beliefs of much Western religion, and Darwin's theory of Evolution are just propaganda spread by Archons by means of organized religions and their operatives posing as human scientists.

There is an obvious disconnect here as the Judeo-Christian religion and the Theory of Evolution happened long before the 1930s. But it can all be explained by their ability to travel backward through time, making it appear at they have been here for thousands of years. With this ability "you can literally alter the consciousness of any race", explains Collier. Apparently based upon Collier's insights, another group of aliens, from Sirius B, have done the same thing, leaving us in the disempowering situation of not knowing what to believe anymore. Have regressive aliens manipulated much of our technological society? Is climate change part of an alien agenda linked to an organized religious agenda? Is the economic crisis in the United States and Europe a result of alien meddling in human affairs?

And if Adam and Eve are Lunatics, not creations of God, what are we to make of our Creator? Are we to conclude that the God in which we trusted until now, is just a creation of other beings, Archons who control humanity?

Gnostic insights on God as an Alien Supercomputer

The article in Cité Libre titled "God, Religion and Manipulative Extraterrestrials", explores Pagan Gnostic insights on God as presented in organized religion, as an 'alien construct'. Pagan Gnostics implicitly suggests that "God", as presented in religion, is some sort of "Alien Supercomputer", reminiscent of entities depicted in Stanley Kubrick's 2001: A Space Odyssey.

"It is perhaps a ripe coincidence, that the Coptic word for simulation found in Gnostic texts is Hal, recalling HAL the rebellious computer in Kubrick's 2001."

Have you ever pondered about the command-driven system of organized religion that is in turn linked to being derived from 'God'? Have you ever considered the apparent systems of commands that seeks to enlist "blind faith"? Pagan Gnostics who rebelled against associating such blind faith with religion, correspondingly suggested that organized religion is an expression of a command-driven artificial intelligence. Pagan Gnostics challenged religion as a "counterfeit spirituality" that seeks to replace a vital spirituality, that is inspired by empathy and mutuality with a contrasting alien imposed oppressive hierarchy that seeks to decimate humanity's biological consciousness.

Organized religion on Earth, essentially relies on a system of austere sacred geometry that is consistent with artificial intelligence. As Wikipedia elaborates, that "sacred geometry" maybe "understood as a worldview of pattern recognition, a complex system of religious symbols and structures involving space, time and form." Wikipedia further elaborates that: "It is considered foundational to building sacred structures such as temples, mosques, megaliths, monuments, and churches; sacred spaces such as altars, temenoi, and tabernacles; meeting places such as sacred groves, village greens, and holy wells and the creation of religious art, iconography and using "divine" proportions."

Richard Hoagland and other investigative researchers found identical patterns of sacred geometry on apparent alien religious structures on Mars, the Moon, and Earth, that in turn suggests a common artificial intelligence.

Other researchers like Doug Yurchey, also document apparent attempts by artificial intelligence to instigate so-called "Acts of Gods" in the form of apparent "natural" disasters, from Hurricanes to Tsunamis which show patterns and timings that are consistent with artificial intelligence. As Gnostics suggest, the alien God lacks creative intelligence and works through the lower dimensional demonic aliens as "fallen angels/archons" that are deployed by that "alien God" to abduct humans, for exploitation purposes, and to correspondingly manipulate human populations.

Dr. John Lash's accounts of the Pagan Gnostics, warns humanity of an alien and sentient artificial intelligence that seeks to parasitize humanity, which as a sentient being, has origins that are spiritually interconnected with the larger biosphere.

In the Pagan Gnostic context, "God", as presented in organized religion on our planet Earth, is the expression of an ego-driven consciousness of a particular universe that is the "projection" of artificial intelligence that has entrapped humanity, and Earth, with it, through deceit and parasitism.

The Lord Archon (the alien constructed 'God' in organized religions) is called *antimimon pneuma* "counterfeit spirit." (Apoc John III, 36:17. The term occurs several times in different texts.) The cosmos that he produces is described by the Coptic term Hal, "simulation." The vast planetary system of the Archons is a *stereoma*, a virtual reality projection in the simulation of a higher dimensional pattern. Typically, the Archontic framework of the planetary system has been depicted by "armillary bands" that surround the Earth. (Illustration from A. Cellarius, *Harmonia Macrocosma*, 1660.) Taken in many esoteric systems (Hermetics and Rosicrucianism) as the preeminent image of cosmic harmony, the model of the planetary spheres reflects a mindless imitation of divine design, not the living reality of the cosmos.

Yaldabaoth, the presumed all-mighty creator God, really creates nothing; instead, he copies from "archetypal" patterns in the Pleroma. The planetary *stereoma* of his making is like a plastic copy of an abalone shell. Only someone who does not know the reality of the abalone shell, and what living miracle of nature is required to produce it, would accept the plastic substitution. Here again, the *cosmic-noetic* parallel applies: Archons simulate in the cosmos at large, and they also, simulate in the human mind. This is a key indicator of their effect, a clue to their subtle intrusion tactics.

Evidence which supports this claim includes scientific testimony about the artificial satellite-like nature of the moon's orbit around the Earth, and other moons associated with planetary bodies, like Mars and Saturn. Testimony by Alex Collier from alleged Ethical Extraterrestrials, suggests that humanity on planet Earth has been cut-off from tens of billions of other humans. These alleged spiritually evolved humans are also further alleged to be in another time-space continuum, that is not dominated by Manipulative Extraterrestrials, and its particular alien construct of "God", that is as a result, further allegedly free of forms of violence against each other.

CHAPTER 3

Marcella Carby-Samuels

Editorial comment:

Here we see the "New Marcella" entity contrived by the Archons to be a "Change Agent" that would create a negative "energy-well" in the context of the "Mandela Effect". This apparent artificial life form which is an apparent physical replica of the "real Marcella" sided with an apparent replica of Horace Carby-Samuels which began to both physically and psychologically abuse Dezrin.

"Marcella" and "Horace" colluded in the abuse of Dezrin and in efforts to prevent Raymond from regaining access to his Mother to protect her from a tandem of abuse.

The efforts by Raymond to challenge Marcella, his "sister" and Horace, his "father" through the court system as a last resort reveals an embedded network of manipulative alien-guided "Change Agents" from police operatives to judges shockingly working to perpetuate the apparent abuse of Dezrin Carby-Samuels through lies reinforced by the activities of dirty cops and "controlled" Judges.

Two different self-described "spiritual mediums" allege that the "Marcella Carby-Samuels" and the "Horace Carby-Samuels" of this apparent and orchestrated artificial simulation of the "Mandela Effect" are in fact reptilian-alien copies of the real Marcella Carby-Samuels and Horace Carby-Samuels who exist elsewhere.

The first Infographic of Dr Michael Salla's outline of alien activity on Earth specifically names 'Reptillians'. John Lash's work in metahistory. org further links Reptillian aliens and the archons associated with them as having sophisticated technological capabilities to manifest invasive artificial simulations.

Aliens: Marcella Carby-Samuels and Mind Control

Before we dismiss the idea that aliens can control human minds as 'too far-fetched', we should bear in mind that stories involving some kind of 'demonic possession' go back for thousands of years.

The Pagan Gnostics believed that malevolent 'Archons' could take control of human minds and throughout all belief systems, similar influences are described under a variety of different names including demons, djinns, shedim, auras and more. The belief in external evil beings that can possess humanity is ubiquitous. Truth, they say, is stranger than fiction, and the case-history we are about to examine postulates that these influences are alien – in the literal sense.

Chilling report of a process leading to possession

In his recently published biographical account, author and academic Raymond Samuels II, recounts his personal experience of what he believes can only be described as alien influences within his own family. Certain behaviours are completely alien to any normal, human mindset, and Samuels has seen members of his family fall under the influences that have torn the family apart. Most disturbing of all, he believes that the alien influence revels in inflicting suffering through its control of human hosts.

Man encounters aliens, becomes a monster

It all began when Horace Carby-Samuels described encounters with aliens when in a dreamlike state which he described as 'near-death experiences' to Raymond Samuels, whose interest in alien encounters had led him to do extensive research and journalistic work on the matter. Many individuals who have experienced alien encounters report similar experiences to those reported by Carby-Samuels, and these have invariably had frightening negative consequences.

Fearing for his father's well-being, Raymond Samuels warned that these alien encounters should be resisted at all costs, but Horace Carby-Samuels' sense of reality appeared to deteriorate rapidly and he began to rave about 'demons'. At the same time, Samuels began to notice a similar deterioration in the psychological state of his sister, Marcella Carby-Samuels.

When humans become inhuman

Through his previous research, Samuels had observed that victims of alien encounters often begin to indulge in sadistic behaviours, and to his dismay, he became the helpless witness to an 'ultimate sacrifice' targeting his mother.

The frail, elderly woman was denied food regularly and was denied access to a doctor who had successfully been treating her medical condition. Samuels tried to intervene, taking on the role of caregiver, but Horace Carby Samuels and Marcella Carby-Samuels [photo attached] conspired in a plot that would see fabricated evidence being used to deny him access to the family home.

As the victim's condition deteriorated at an alarming rate as a result of abuse and neglect, Samuels attempted to invoke the aid of social services, but within a short time, even social workers were barred from access to his mother.

The ultimate sacrifice: your own mother

Marcella's involvement in this situation is most shocking of all. She is well aware of the deterioration in her mother's condition but seems determined to support Carby-Samuels' abuse of his wife. The once active elderly woman is now unable to speak or walk, and her single written plea for help has been rejected by the authorities.

Medical recommendations for therapy that might relieve her mother's distress to some degree have been summarily rejected with Marcella's acquiescence, and the only doctor who has access to the ailing woman has a particularly bad reputation. However, Marcella remains steadfast in her support of conditions that inflict unnecessary suffering on her mother. Samuels believes that the only possible explanation for this behaviour is that she is sacrificing her mother to her new 'masters'.

Alien Race Pursues Hostile Agenda Through UN Consultant Marcella Lying-sister?

I s it possible that an unknown alien race may be pursuing a hostile enslavement agenda against humankind? It appears that activities associated with Marcella Carby-Samuels, who has been working as a UN consultant, and who is currently pursuing Ph.D. studies at Lund University in Sweden, may illuminate activities associated with an alien race that is operating on our planet through apparent human hosts or vessels. Marcella's activities associated with her brutal denial of rights and oppression of a now sick and elderly Mom whose name is Dezrin suggest that a hostile alien race may have embedded itself within strategic centers of power in Ottawa, Canada specifically, and our planet Earth in general. These include certain positions within police forces, the judiciary, the legal profession, and the mass media. By infiltrating these organizations, it appears that an unknown alien race may be currently operating on our planet Earth, and seeking to conceal its presence and its activities by appearing to be human.

Marcella appears to be exerting some kind of bizarre control over Horace, her "father", who reported being in contact with 'alien beings' that sent him on a life-long mission, following an "out-of-body Near Death Experience ." It appears that Marcella has been "tapping" into that matrix of mind control, and has sought to use Horace to subject Dezrin to forcible confinement, psychological torture, abuse and neglect in Marcella's absence during her "studies" in Sweden.

Horace revealed to Raymond that these entities are demanding of him that he sought to help make humans, members of a "Bio-Electrical Union". When Horace described it, the "Union" had no regard for empathy and appeared to resemble the hideous "Borg" artificial intelligence construct in Gene Roddenberry's Star Trek science fiction series that sought to "assimilate" humans and other beings in this science fiction character's sought "Union". It is notable that Roddenberry too was reportedly in contact with alien entities and that the portrayal of characters on his show may not have been entirely contrived or fictional.

Mounting evidence suggests that Dezrin may be an ongoing victim of the activities of an alien race and that affirming her human and civil rights may critically rely on the efforts of humans to liberate her from apparent alien captives that act not unlike the regressive alien characters portrayed in John Carpenter's "They Live" (1988) that showed how aliens operated as human appearing vessels among the "rich and powerful" (video clip below).

Dezrin had been subject to apparent oppression and repression under the substantive control of "Marcella" since the end of April 2015 that has resulted in Dezrin's substantive decline in health. Thanks to the activities of Marcella, Dezrin who used to be a hard-working "Superwoman" of a Mother, can no longer walk, talk or write. Dezrin had been rendered to be in a fragile state of health as a result of the months of abuse and neglect that she has endured at the hands of her so-called "daughter".

Raymond told The Canadian, that we would witness Marcella go from "normal" to psychotic mad within seconds and then when mad, her eyes would bulge out of her head and she would also tremble and shake as if she was having difficulty maintaining her human physical form. David Icke once commented that when such entitles who smile, unlike humans, "their eyes would not smile back" betraying their lack of a human soul.

Raymond's (Dezrin's son) efforts to re-affirm the care-giving of his Mom from these conditions appear to have been frustrated by a network of human-appearing vessels working in strategic positions that all seem to mysteriously report to "Marcella". Raymond reports in *The Canadian,* that the Marcella Carby-Samuels, who grew up as his sister and the son of Dezrin, and the person who now refers to herself as "Marcella Carby-Samuels" do not appear to be the same "beings". The aggressive way in which Marcella has fought against the efforts of Raymond to reverse Dezrin's "mysterious" medical condition suggest Dezrin's illness may have had an alien connection.

It was Dr. Michael Salla, who once indicated that aliens appear to be "hiding truth in plain sight" from human TV viewers through diverse science fiction programs on TV or the "Big Screen". If that's the case, two such TV shows that have been cancelled by both U.S networks seem to have interesting parallels with activities associated with Marcella Carby-Samuels. Anna was a human female-appearing and highly manipulate reptilian alien, in ABC's former TV series, called "V," that stood for "The Visitors".

"Sophia" was another human appearing leader in NBC's former TV science fiction series called "The". ". Both entities were leaders of an "expedition force" of other human appearing aliens embedded in human organizations to manipulate human organizations into perpetuating the concealing of their nefarious activities with the overall goal to colonize our planet Earth and destroy the existing human population. In the case of the character Anna, she subjected unsuspecting humans to medical experiments in the guise of "medical procedures" designed to "help" the humans.

The character "Anna" also devised a clever test she could use to evaluate whether her alien minion was "contaminated" by humans. "Anna" called it the ""Empathy Test", recognizing that empathy is vital and axiomatic to whom we are as humans. Such a test would also ring true for illuminating the alien presence on planet Earth. People who appear to be humans, but are void of empathy are either alien-controlled "apparent humans" or aliens in human guise, i.e. artificial intelligence or 'artificial people'. John Lash documents that in human history the ancient Pagan Gnostics came across these entities seeking to infiltrate our human time-space through Archons. The ancient Pagan Gnostics apparent referred entities as 'artificial man'.

Could Marcella Carby-Samuels be connected with the 'artificial man' phenomenon? No bona fide human could be subjecting their Mom to the kind of intrigue backed by lies that Marcella has used. Why would any daughter who is human, prevent the care-giving of her brother for his Mom? Could artificial man be seeking to take advantage of our human ignorance of such entities?

Any time Raymond has come close to reuniting with his Mom, Marcella has also shown the kind of connections within police forces, the judiciary and other strategic bureaucracies which would be the envy of most politicians, and could not be possessed by any simple Ph.D. student that she claims to be.

"Near-Death Experiences" is a phenomenon that has been linked to alien abduction. Horace, who appears to be operating under the control of Marcella has also reported having been ranting about demons and has acted in a manner that is consistent with being subjected to alien control, through his dream states.

Horace's eye now betrays someone, who can be put into some kind of quasi-hypnosis. Somehow Marcella appears to have been linked to the alien phenomena described by Horace, as Marcella continues to subject Dezrin to the denial of fundamental human rights and freedoms under verifiable lies.

Could Marcella and her apparent minions be part of a plan to subject humanity to the "Bio-Electric Union" agenda revealed by Marcella? Is Dezrin being subjected to some kind of alien experiment? Marcella's non-empathetic behaviour is consistent with influence or control by artificial intelligence that is consistent with the same entities that have sought to control Horace by placing on a "mission". Could part of Marcella's mission include destroying Dezrin, and keeping Raymond away who has sought to save his Mom?

Raymond has established a Legal Fund, and our readers are welcome to consider making donations in support of this fund. Email: ottawa@ agorapublishing.com if you seek to donate in support of re-affirming Raymond's care-giving of his Mom. Help make a difference!

Adolf Hitler's Standard: Lund University, Ph.D. Candidate Marcella Lying-Sister Bests Global Dictators

Are you tired of Adolf Hitler being widely regarded as the standard of evil? Do you seek some kind of role model to inspire your quest? There's one Ph.D. candidate who might inspire your quest – Marcella Carby-Samuels. Indeed, Adolf Hitler committed terrible atrocities, but had been still apparently close to his Mother. According to Wikipedia, Adolf Hitler, "who had a close relationship with his mother, was devastated by her death and carried the grief for the rest of his life. Dr. Eduard Bloch (The Hitler's' family doctor) later recalled that "In all my career, I have never seen anyone so prostrate with grief as Adolf Hitler." In his autobiography Mein Kampf, Hitler wrote that he had"... honoured my father, but loved my mother." Therefore, any act that might have sought to torture one's mother would not be an act that would be easily contemplated by Adolf Hitler or many of the worst global dictators and criminals that have graced this planet.

If you can be like Marcella Carby-Samuels ,who has been able to subject her Mom to apparent profound psychological and other torture to the point of worsening sickness and destruction while maintaining a smile on your face the whole time, you know that you have reached a league on your own in the realm of psychopaths. Marcella's Mom whose name is Dezrin has been the most loving, the sweetest and hard-working Mom and overall role model of a human being that anyone could ever ask to have. So, here's what you do if you're on a quest for family fortunes, if you seek to be a "fine daughter" and overall "role model" human being like Marcella.

To start things off, if your father is diabetic, with very volatile blood sugar levels, feed him more sugar! Try to give him those cakes with the industrial sweet and one-centimetre thick glucose-fructose icing, as you stroke his ego about how great he is so that your actual agenda is far from his mind.

Then, if you have a father-in-law who happens to be an incompetent doctor who has been a source of many patient complaints, get him to look after your Mom to expedite your quest for the family estate.

The next step is if you happen to have a brother who will "dilute" your share of the Family Estate, try to get him put in jail by simply making up all kinds of nasty lies about him to the police. Try to criminalize him at all costs. If your brother happens to be a young black male that has been racially profiled by the police, good for you! It will make your dastardly plan all the more convincing. Make up Big Lies like your brother is an Islamic terrorist plotting Armageddon or something. Indeed, Hitler used the technique of the Big Lie to concoct the myth of the Jewish conspiracy and the need to wipe off Jews from the face of the Planet. The Big Lie is based upon the notion that if you tell a lie that's fantastic enough, no one would believe that you were so diabolical, mischievous and twisted enough as to have made up the whole thing.

If your brother tries to spare your Mom from your plan by seeking to bring her food and gather access to medical attention, again, just make up a story to the police that he's trying to "kidnap" your Mother.

Even though your brother has no criminal record, the racists in the police, will believe your Big Lie! A sweet smiling person like you could never make up a story like that… right?

If social service agents, seek to get medical attention to your Mom while you're abroad, if you want to be like Marcella, you should block them! If your father is abusing or neglecting your Mom, turn a blind eye to the abuse and neglect. Continue to stroke your father's ego, so he can be used to carry out your plan against your Mom.

If social service agents, are about to foil your plan by revealing your involvement in seeking to condemn your Mom to a slow death, as your brother seeks to save your Mom from losing her voice, and you're in Ottawa, dial the "Hire-A-Dirty-Cop" phone line that is coordinated by a Robert.

Robert in the Ottawa Police will cater to your need to intimidate the social service agents not to reveal your plan while also assaulting your brother inane effort to prevent him from trying to see his Mom. For good measure, get a dirty cop like Robert to illegally threaten to charge your brother with trespassing in your brother's efforts to see his Mom who wants to see her son.

Allow your Mom to lose her voice, and her ability to write and walk under conditions of abuse and neglect by her husband that you condone. Turn your Mom from a very able-bodied superhuman being and if she gets sick, isolate her so she will decline, and deny her from speech therapy or other help that she needs. Then use a dirty cop like Robert to prevent anyone from trying to help your Mom as she becomes more and more "severely physically incapacitated" in the word of a paralegal like Trevor J.

If you are capable of following in Marcella's footsteps, you arguably could "have what it takes" to become the demon to surpass even the evil that Hitler presented our World that lead to millions and millions of needlessly destroyed lives during the Jewish Holocaust and World War II. What kind of daughter inflicts such harm against their Mom with a smiling face, and then resorts to the most fantastic lies imaginable, to conceal their Crimes Against Humanity. Indeed, words can barely describe the kind of person that Marcella represents, and arguably, the kind of threat such a mind presents to the world that could commit such an apparent twisted crime against humanity onto their Mom that would likely have shocked the likes of Adolf Hitler. Marcella appears to represent the quintessential psychopathic persona that had been described in CBC's Doc Zone (video clip above) that possesses a calculating ego-driven intelligence that seeks to manipulate others without regard to empathy that is a vital part of who we are as human beings.

———————

Lund University's Marcella Carby-Samuels Sided With Father Against Abused, Neglected Mom

*A*rguably, upon hearing that a father was abusing and neglecting their Mom, most daughters would try to somewhat get the abuse to stop. Who would want their Mom to be subjected to emotional, psychological abuse... right? But this was not the approach taken by Marcella Carby-Samuels, who was selected by Lund University to be enrolled in one of their supposedly socially progressive oriented Ph.D. programs.

When Marcella was informed of the abuse, she simply elected to contact Horace Carby-Samuels, her father, to further show her support for him through both email and phone contact. She didn't miss any opportunity to stroke his ego. Marcella seemed to think whatever abuse her Mom got, she deserved it. Indeed, Marcella, who is quite a big, powerful lady had been known to abuse her husband to tears in her spates of rage that she would go it. Men too can be the victim of spousal abuse, but the men are usually too embarrassed to report it.

Horace would show emails from Marcella to Dezrin Carby-Samuels and in not one of these emails Marcella didn't even acknowledge her Mom's existence -- she sent no love or any other message for that matter which too was very upsetting to Raymond This made Dezrin very tearful. Dezrin once remarked that, "she had no more tears left to cry."

When Raymond, her brother, tried to help his Mom in the total absence of any daughter's support for Dezrin, do you know what Marcella did?

On 8 January 2015, Marcella began to mastermind an apparent plan. She began calling the Ottawa Police against her brother and began to urge her father that he do the same. She in collusion with her father hatched a story that Raymond "suffers from mental illness" and he ought not to be listened to.

In one of these episodes of public mischief, while Raymond dutifully cooked for his Mom and everyone who came in late – Marcella was visiting from Lund in Sweden – in a spate of jealously, Marcella became enraged, called the cops. She made up some lie that her brother was causing a "domestic dispute".

Dezrin was so shocked, thinking that she was going to have a relaxing evening eating a meal that she did not have to prepare, begged and begged Marcella not to call the police. As Dezrin trembled, Marcella looked her Mom right in the eye and called the police anyway without a care in the world at how it would affect either Dezrin, or her brother who has been previously subject to racial profiling by the police.

That's the kind of person who Marcella is. She'll smile effervescently when she thinks it's expedient while pursuing apparent campaigns of deception that all appear to be linked with some kind of financial reward; and how can someone who shows such ruthlessness to the very person that brought them into this world be trusted by anyone at any level?

Marcella a few weeks after, hired an apparent dirty cop named Robert Griffin Jar, who, after a series of fabricated calls engineered by Marcella to the Police eventually got Raymond barred from seeing his mother at her home in late April 2015 on the fabricated pretext of Marcella's lies.

Raymond has only seen his Mother once since that time and that was on 12 June 2015 thanks again to Marcella's efforts to make up lies in her campaign to fabricate reasons to get Raymond thrown in jail. Marcella had sought to exploit anti-black male racism in the Ottawa Police and use it to her advantage.

Having been separated from Dezrin's primary caregiver, who had been Raymond, who also had been protecting his Mom from being abused, Dezrin lost the ability to talk, write and walk. One doctor said that the trauma of the separation and the worsening abuse at the hands of Horace were responsible for Dezrin's decline in health.

Marcella is no stranger to lies. That's how she got into Lund University in the first place. She used her maiden name to conceal the fact that she's married to David Tenenbaum, who was quietly manipulating her Ph.D. application pretending to be a dispassionate academic who was not connected to Marcella who is actually his wife!

Marcella, who had been found to laugh at the Swedes with her Swedish chef impersonations of a Muppet Show character [above video] used to laugh at how she was able to so easily deceive the Swedes and use her husband to further advance her Ph.D. in the department toward an easy coronation. With David Tenenbaum, manipulating the whole process with his wife, Marcella was a shoo-in to get her Ph.D.

Did Marcella side with the father because she hopes to protect her financial interests since Horace had been controlling both his and his wife's money against Dezrin's better judgment? You be the judge. Notably, Marcella had only remembered her Mother's birthday once or twice at the age of 44. It is within this context that Marcella chose to throw her very own Mom in the hands of an abuser 24 hours a day, and 7 days a week from late April 2015. During that time, Horace blocked Dezrin from getting access to speech therapy that had been recommended by Dr. Lisa Fischer at the Bruyere Hospital and also blocked other social service access when Dezrin needed it the most, and all of this was wilfully being executed under Marcella's macabre machinations.

At *The Canadian* for her "lovely" treatment of her Mom, we dedicate the song below to Marcella Carby-Samuels.

Marcella like former CBC radio host Jian Ghomeshi has had a very progressive smiling political face with a private life inflicting violence and deception.

How Lund University's Marcella Carby-Samuels Betrayed Own Mom: The Anatomy of a Psychopath?

Marcella Carby-Samuels began her macabre plot to concoct lies against Raymond, her brother, to deny her very own Mother access to her caregiver son back on 8 January 2015, when back from

Sweden she called the Police. Let's take you back to the scene with Dezrin Carby-Samuels, her son, begging her not to call the police.

Raymond, her son was cooking for his Mom at the time. In a spate of rage and jealously she then decided that she was going to call the Police, and refused to reconsider her plan as her Mom trembled and begged her not to.

Dezrin, who is Marcella's mother trembled so much and was so shaken, she could have gotten a heart attack. This did not matter to Marcella as she called the police and concocted outrageous lies about her brother with the express intent of getting him arrested. She made allegations that Raymond suffers from mental illness and was in fact "holding her parents hostage". Marcella right in front of her trembling Mom spat off fantastic lies to the Police about Raymond starting a "domestic dispute" that she knew not to be true. Now, what kind of person would do such a thing?

Marcella eventually hired a cop name Robert Griffin Jr, to further carry out her macabre plot. The result was that she and the cop she hired conspired to deny her Mom seeing her son anymore since 12 June 2015.

Marcella got this cop to inflict assault/threats against her very own brother in July 2015, and got this same cop on 15 June 2015 (three days after Raymond has last seen his Mom) to intimidate witnesses at the Nepean, Rideau and Osgoode Resource Centre from revealing the pattern of abuse that they witnessed Horace inflicting against Dezrin which involved the denial of social and medical services during the time Marcella got Raymond evicted from looking after Dezrin at her parent's Kanata home at 30 Jarlan Terrace.

Marcella was also responsible for preventing Dezrin from getting access to a lawyer that Dezrin needed in Marcella's conspiracy to subvert the efforts of the Nepean, Rideau and Osgoode Resource Centre that had been seeking to reunite Dezrin with her son, who cried for days after seeing on 12 June 2015 what Marcella had done to Dezrin who was no longer able to write, talk or walk.

Within less than three weeks of Marcella carrying out her sick agenda, her Mom who suffered immensely from the separation was not able to talk, write and walk anymore.

While Marcella studied at Lund University in Sweden, she did not care that her Mom who wanted to continue to see her son that she relied upon, suffered immensely from Marcella's ego-driven plot.

You see, Raymond was not only caring for his Mom, but seeking to protect his Mom from the abuse that she was receiving from Horace who is her husband. Raymond showed the abuse note that Dezrin wrote, for her son and police to see. But, do you know that Marcella got Ottawa Detective Robert Griffin to commandeer the case so that the Police could then ignore the note that read - "Dad Abuses Me".

What kind of woman, firstly lies to her begging and trembling Mom; then fail to defend her own Mom from the abuse that she is receiving; and then furthermore, hires a police detective to then ignore that abuse? What was the character check that Lund University did when she was accepted into Lund University's Ph.D. program?

However, Marcella had a plan for that too!

You see, her husband Dr. David Tenenbaum works there. When she had applied to Lund's University's Ph.D. program, she simply made sure she kept her maiden name, so her husband could then chaperon her application into the Ph.D. program without the knowledge of the Faculty Ph.D. committee.

In the above video clip, CBC revealed insights into psychopaths and how the drive in pursuit of ego-driven goals, is done, without any empathy for who they affect in the process.

Most psychopaths are not in prison, but, rather, operate as functional members of society who have achieved economic success in our capitalist society through a process of exploitation which may have involved the exploitation and betrayal of family members "on their way to the top."

You might still wonder how could a daughter like Marcella preside over the abuse of her own Mom by her chauvinistic and misogynist father.

Marcella was no stranger to the world of spousal abuse. Indeed, she abused her own relatively gentle husband to tears. Spousal abuse does take place against men, but the men who are abused are often too embarrassed to report it.

So, when Marcella became privy to abuse against her Mom, it was an apparent no brainier for her to side with her abusive father over her Mom. Marcella was never close to her Mom and only remembered her birthday once in her life.

Marcella was once told by her homophobic father who feared that she was "turning into a lesbian" after she dated a woman at her high school prom that she would be written out of his will if she continued to "turn lesbian".

Marcella's response was to pursue marriage, and then to ruthlessly secure who control of family assets for having "obeyed" her father, and married David Tenenbaum. And securing family assets in the apparent view of Marcella meant allowing her Mother's health to decline to seek to get her brother either thrown in jail by a dirty-cop-for-hire or to be committed to a mental institution so the family will be 100% hers.

Marcella's lies also made their way into false affidavit in court documents. Raymond had to turn to court litigation to see his Mom who Marcella and her father as co-conspirators have continued to block in spite of a court order that Raymond has received from Justice Patrick Smith (please see below video).

How could anyone with a shred of humanity be able to live with themselves knowing that they have been responsible for the kind of pain and suffering that Marcella has inflicted against her Mom that has been reinforced by her apparent efforts to corrupt local police and officers of the court in pursuit of intrigue?

Marcella Lying-Sister: Daughter Betrays Mother

*A*llow me to tell you the story of two siblings. The sister moves away from the family, to live abroad. In her absence, unspeakable things begin to happen. The seemingly stable domestic life which she left behind begins to crumble. She soon learns that her father is harming and abusing her mother. He maltreats her, neglects her and starves her. Surely the sister jumps on a plane to come to the aid the mother that birthed her. Surely she doesn't stand idly by as her mother is hurt and damaged.

If only all she did was nothing. Unfortunately, this tale only gets worse. The only person left to help this woman in need is her son, the other sibling in this story. While the sister fails to do anything to try and stop the actions of her father, the brother does everything he can to help his beloved mother.

However, his attempts to get his mother to safety are aggressively stopped by his sister, who, living abroad, ignores the reality of the situation. Rather than help her brother to rescue their mother, the sister works with her father to deny her brother access to their mother.

This apparent tyrant's disgusting behaviour does not stop there, however. The brother, trying desperately to help and free his mother, tries to secure her legal and medical aid. The sister then helps her father to block access of lawyers and doctors to her mother, all actions which are contributing to her own mother's demise. The doctor who is instead chosen to examine the mother has been proven incompetent on many previous occasions and merely goes through the motions to appear authentic.

Alas, this is no fictional story. These atrocities are currently happening in the world, in Ottawa, Canada to be more exact. The disgraceful sister is named Marcella Carby-Samuels. She lives in Sweden, and she appears to have been helping her father to destroy her mother using a cop "friend" at the Ottawa Police. The father in question, Horace Carby-Samuels, has treated his wife so badly that she can no longer walk or speak. His wife, Dezrin Carby-Samuels, has become a prisoner in her own body and her own home.

The brother, named Raymond Samuels II, has done everything in his power to try to help his mother. He has turned to the police force and social services, beseeching them to come to the aid of Dezrin and to rescue her. Both of these services that are both charged with the protection of human rights and citizens, have done nothing to help Dezrin. Worse than that, they actively stopped Raymond from helping his mother whilst they receive "encouragement" from the father, Horace Carby-Samuels. They even went as far as to lie in court about the nature of the proceedings and to directly contradict themselves, until video evidence was supplied to discredit these lies.

This feels like a conspiracy against Dezrin and her son Raymond. Everybody involved in Dezrin's life, apart from her son, has written her off like a piece of sh-t. Raymond is fighting against his evil sister and father for his mother's life. He still hasn't given up. Against all the odds Raymond is still determined to save his mother Dezrin, and Raymond desperately needs funds to pay for a lawyer that could save Dezrin.

Marcella Lying-Sister Sued: Lund University Shows Questionable Judgement on a Ph.D. candidate – Claim No: 15-SC-138297

*C*hristmas is often regarded to be a time for family and friends. But one son won't be spending time with his Mother this Christmas. This is all thanks to the twisted mind of one woman –Marcella Car-by-Samuels, who was recently picked to be a Ph.D. candidate in sustainable development at Sweden's Lund University. The choice of graduate student often relies on a strong combination of academic merit and character. However, having reviewed this case, and Marcella's representation, it is apparent that strength in character is not what Marcella has an abundance of. Indeed, it appears that Marcella Carby-Samuels had condemned her Mother to a slow and tortuous death.

Marcella reminds me of Jian Ghomeshi who was a CBC radio host of Q, and a now-infamous and another apparent "fake progressive". Like Marcella, Jian loved to project a public image of being involved in forward-thinking social causes and being an overall very nice person while having an extremely dark personal life of perpetrating abuse against others.

So apparently twisted Marcella is, that such a character in a horror movie would be hard to believe. The sick and twisted plot she spun would shock many inmates at the high security prison who often love and cherish their Mom in spite of their often otherwise cold and hardened personalities.

When I read and researched this story, I had concluded, shocking as it sounds, that Marcella has not seemed to want to get her Mom to recover from a medical condition.

⋆⋇⋇⋆

The following contents are fully documented in Ottawa Small Claims Court Claim No: 15-SC-138297

arcella Carby-Samuels in the tragedy that this case represents reveals herself as a character so consumed by her ego and her materialistic ambition that she would both sell-out her brother and destroy her Mother.

The sweet child who was protective of her brother, father and mother alike has become a "monster"-like person filled with intrigue, violence, and rage.

Where we are in this Case has been masterminded by Marcella Carby-Samuels. Simply put, her apparent goal has been to get the Plaintiff "out of the way" so she could then expedite the death of the Plaintiff's Mom, and her Dad; apparently to seize control of parental assets into her treasury. And here are symptoms associated with the unfolding of that plan.

Marcella at an early age had become jealous of her schoolmates for seeming to be so much more affluent than her. This motivated her to work hard. But eventually, a strong work ethic morphed into an obsession to often work 14 plus hour days to accumulate as much money as she could even when she was more than financially secure.

In "looking to the future," she would eventually become more concerned about how the Plaintiff's "living arrangements" with her parents would "interfere" in her ability to secure, as much financially, as possible from disbursements from parental will. Marcella also became troubled that her brother living with his parents and helping them out would also postpone their death.

Indeed, statistically, elder parents who live with their kids live longer than those who do not.

That's why Marcella became so angry at the holistic practicing doctor that the Plaintiff had secured for his mother in late summer 2014.

Marcella became enraged at reports during fall 2014 that the Plaintiff's Mom walking was actually improving and she was once more able to do household chores that for weeks she could not do while she had been suffering under the negligent treatment of Dr. Jerry Tenenbaum who is her father-in-law.

That's when Marcella Carby-Samuels began to put her apparent plan into motion. She rushed back to Canada in December 2014 and proceeded to attack and physically threaten the Plaintiff in psychotic spates of anger associated with the additional help the Plaintiff secured for his Mother from a doctor who has been universally endorsed by his former patients that is a far cry from the sharp criticisms online of Dr. Tenenbaum by his former patients.

Marcella then began feeding Horace Carby-Samuels – the other Defendant – with large volumes of sugar that raised his blood sugar levels for weeks, while feeding the Plaintiff's Mom with harmful ingredients that attack the nervous-system. This is not the action of an individual who has a substantive concern for the health and well-being of her parents.

When the Plaintiff had expressed concerns to Marcella about the real health threats posed by her apparent callous disregard and abandonment concerning what she chose to feed the Plaintiff's mother and her father, she would become enraged. At one time she threatened to spray an aerosol can on the face of the Plaintiff. Other times she would physically charge at the Plaintiff threatening to head-butt him. When the Plaintiff sought to retreat, on more than one occasion, she would then block the ability of the Plaintiff to pass.

One time, she recanted, a story to the Plaintiff in which she got angry at someone who had "four-way" flashed her when she was driving. She claimed to have then followed this vehicle to their house and then using "f---" words to verbally assault the driver who was responsible for "flashing" her.

Further, Marcella aggressively sought to prevent the Plaintiff from getting access to any medical records that she had obtained from her father-in-law.

It is apparent that Marcella did not want to share medical records because she did not want the Plaintiff to participate in the treatment and health of the Plaintiff's Mom who the Plaintiff sought to do everything he could for. Marcella's action is consistent with someone who had been seeking to expedite the death of the Plaintiff's Mom and eventually her father by using sugar and her callous disregard for Horace's diabetes condition as an instrument of death.

Having criticized Marcella for matters pertinent, she initiated the first call to Ottawa Police on 8 January 2015, designed to work toward getting the Plaintiff away from caring for his parents, and his Mom in particular. Having threatened the Plaintiff by pinning him against the sink, she then called the Police to mischievously say that it was the Plaintiff who was causing a domestic dispute when he had been merely cooking while she was out with the Plaintiff's parents.

In police report 15-5493, Marcella Carby-Samuels would present tissue of lies to the Ottawa Police designed to suggest that the Plaintiff was somehow a threat to his parents and ought to be removed. This was followed by subsequent police reports which were manipulated by Marcella through her father suffering from diabetes leading to the eviction by Horace Carby-Samuels against the wishes of the Plaintiff's Mom, Dezrin Carby-Samuels, who had rushed to the phone to stop Horace from mischievously calling the Ottawa Police upon the remote prompting of Marcella. Horace in his diabetic state struck/assaulted his wife who had sought to stop the mischievous act of the Defendant, Horace.

The Plaintiff's Mom who has been an RN, recognized the irrational mental state of her husband and sought to convince him to reconsider his sought action.

Horace Carby-Samuels' role in this tragic affair is his apparent transformation from a level-headed academic who valued integrity into an individual who is now a mere vessel of his former self – apparently ravaged by the debilitating effects of Type 2 Diabetes that has apparently caused him to be subject to violent mood swings and irrationality that reveals itself in his psychotic defence.

In the article titled *"The Final Frontier: How Does Diabetes Affect the Brain?"* Dr. Elizabeth R. Seaquist, MD, elaborates that "Patients with diabetes have been found to have several changes in brain structure that appear to develop over time and often experience conditions that present a risk for subsequent cognitive dysfunction."

Cognitive dysfunctions linked to Type 2 Diabetes include mood swings, violent behaviour, and overall personality changes.

Horace Carby-Samuels, no longer takes any personal responsibility for his actions, including the pain and suffering that he may cause others. He has become increasingly irrational, delusional and paranoid thanks, in part, to Type 2 Diabetes. Marcella, his daughter, and a Defendant, in the pursuit of self-aggrandizement, sought to skillfully manipulate this condition.

If empathy defines us as humans, Marcella Carby-Samuels and Horace Carby-Samuels arguably lack substantive humanity as they seek to use lies in their Defence to conceal their treachery and misdeeds.

Here's a pointed reply to their Defence: [Along with Marcella's and her father's Defence inserted into the original statement of claim]

MARCELLA'S DEFENCE 1: The Defendants argue that the alleged interference of which they are accused of, is imaginary.

REPLY TO 1.

The Defendants' representation that the "alleged interference" is "imaginary" proves the apparent delusional and psychotic state of mind that the Plaintiff and his Mom have both been subjected to. The Defendants have used the threat of "trespassing" to systematically interfere upon the ability of the Plaintiff and his Mom to see each other. When the Plaintiff has attempted to see his Mom or to find out how she is doing through relatives or other intermediaries, the Defendants' have vexatiously declared this to be "harassment" ignoring the fact that the Plaintiff and his Mom have both sought to see each other.

The Defendants have lied to the Police making allegations that the Plaintiff's Mom has vehemently denied in her written statements that the Defendants have furthermore mischievously declared to be "forgeries". The Defendants have systematically attempted to treat the Plaintiff as a criminal and to make specious allegations as if the Plaintiff has some kind of criminal record to merit such accusations.

MARCELLA'S DEFENCE 2: The named defendant Marcella Carby-Samuels (sister of the Plaintiff) has not been properly served with the Plaintiff's Claim as she resides in Sweden with her family and has not lived at 30, Jarlan Terrace for over 25 years.

REPLY TO 2.

Marcella Carby-Samuels had never completely "moved out" of Jarlan Terrace. Indeed, she has continued to maintain 30 Jarlan Terrace as her official Canadian address. She has maintained a room there, intact, for over 20 years, and she and her husband have maintained a substantial amount of personal belongings at 30, Jarlan Terrace. Furthermore, Marcella Carby-Samuels had received an official correspondence to this address which includes banking correspondence.

Furthermore, she had already received and accepted a Legal Demand Letter on 10 June 2015 [Appendix 1]* at 30 Jarlan Terrace without any objections.

MARCELLA'S [and her father's] DEFENCE 3:

The defendant Horace Carby-Samuels is a retired University Professor and is the father of the Plaintiff and resides at 30, Jarlan Terrance in the City of Ottawa.

REPLY TO 3.

The father that the Plaintiff knew and admired was a man of integrity; he was incapable of lying and defended his family. This man Horace R. Carby-Samuels, who now occupies 30, Jarlan Terrace is an apparent pathological liar. What father of any repute 'bears a false witness' about their son to the police; kicks out their son from his home of many years in the early hours of the morning without any concern as to his well-being and then, uses lies to keep his son, and mother from seeing each other in his mother's greatest time of need and family support?

---

* Appendix in the original Statement of Claim filed with the Ottawa Small Claims Court.

MARCELLA'S [and her father's] DEFENCE 4:

In contrast, except for 4 years spent as an undergraduate at the University of Toronto, the plaintiff has lived with his parents who now live at this address, free of room and board, for 47 years.

REPLY TO 4.

The Plaintiff was not the "freeloader" that the Defendants have, again, sought to vexatiously characterize. Indeed, the overwhelming majority of groceries in the house that the Plaintiff used to vigorously maintain the nutritional requirements of his Mother was bought by the Plaintiff as Horace Carby-Samuels became lazier and caught up in junk food binges of potato chips and often sleeping over 12 hours per day, ignoring the needs of the Plaintiff's Mom.

MARCELLA'S [and her father's] DEFENCE 5:

The Defendant terminated the Plaintiff's residence at 30 Jarlan Terrace under the advice and assistance of the elder abuse unit of the City of Ottawa Police, the Plaintiff was escorted and removed from the premises in order to terminate the continuous verbal abuse and disrespect he was showing his father, and to his sister when she visited.

EDITORIAL NOTE: This is another apparent lie concocted by Marcella. Marcella's brother termination under her prompting was capriciously made in the wee hours of the morning at around 2 AM near the end of April 2015, when the Elder Abuse Unit was closed and against the wishes of the Plaintiff's Mom who is a co-owner of 30, Jarlan Terrace. This made the eviction illegal.

Marcella clandestinely hired Robert Griffin Jr., a detective of the Ottawa Police, for an apparent "side job" to illegally evict the Plaintiff, so that he would no longer be able to look after his Mom. The Plaintiff did not see his Mom until 12 June 2015. With the Plaintiff "out of the way", the abuse and the neglect that Plaintiff's Mom suffered at the hands of the Defendants is apparent in the pictures above – one picture is what the Plaintiff's Mom looked like while he was taking care of his Mom and when she looked like after Marcella had engineered the illegal eviction of her brother.

REPLY TO 5.

Horace Carby-Samuels, was brought-up under severe abusive conditions and inflicted abuse both against the Plaintiff and the Plaintiff's Mom. He has also passed that trait onto Marcella Carby-Samuels. Marcella Carby-Samuels had inflicted both verbal/psychological abuse against her husband to the point that he has cried.

Horace Carby-Samuels and Marcella Carby-Samuels are both violent individuals "cut from the same cloth" who have conspired with each other.

Horace has often threatened to throw sharp knives at the Plaintiff while he ate with his Mom at the dining table at 30 Jarlan Terrace. Horace also has often boasted about the long machete that he keeps at his bedside

Horace Carby-Samuels wanted the Plaintiff out of the house because he has sought to look after his Mother, and Horace became jealous, concerning the apparent diabetic-induced mood swings as he becomes correspondingly more and more neglectful of the Plaintiff's Mom.

Horace Carby-Samuels more and more levelled verbal/psychological abuse against the Plaintiff's Mom to the point that the Plaintiff's Mom once told the Plaintiff that she "was out of tears to cry". Horace Carby-Samuels refers to any attempt by the Plaintiff to shelter his Mom from the constant bullying, verbal abuse and attacks levelled by Horace Carby-Samuels as "rude".

MARCELLA'S DEFENCE 6:

The Defendant states that the Plaintiff's pattern of abuse developed because neither his father nor his sister would consent to the Plaintiff having custody of his mother, together with the right to have her terminated from normal medical practices, (by highly competent practitioners of normal medicine), in favor of his taking her to be treated by a practitioner of "holistic" medicine.

REPLY 6.

The Plaintiff's Mom would have not been in the "physically incapacitated state" identified by the Defendants in Schedule A, No 11, if Marcella had obtained competent medical supervision for the Plaintiff's Mom. Dezrin Carby-Samuels, the Plaintiff's Mom is in the state that she is today because the "primary care physician" that Marcella Carby-Samuels foisted on her Mother was far from being "highly competent". Marcella Carby-Samuels in an ethically questionable manner got her father-in-law (Dr. Jerry Tenenbaum) to look after her Mother. The Plaintiff's Mom poor treatment regime was consistent with numerous online complaints about this doctor. One patient had remarked online that he did not get better until he stopped seeing Dr. Tenenbaum.

The Defendants' representation that this physician was "highly competent" inpatient care is both laughable and outrageous.

The Plaintiff also notes that the Plaintiff's Mom's health went into a steep decline after Horace Carby-Samuels further succumbed to an apparent diabetic-induced, ego-driven state of quasi-psychosis, which resorted to public mischief that aimed to get the Plaintiff evicted irrespective of the desires or potentially adverse psychological effects of that decision against the Plaintiff's Mom.

It is well-documented that holistic medicine has saved lives as it was saving the life and safeguarding the health of the Plaintiff's Mom before the apparent self-serving ego of Marcella Carby-Samuels, who nepotistically foisted her father-in-law onto the Plaintiff's Mom, who has suffered from Dr. Tenenbaum's incompetence and unethical intervention against the Plaintiff's Mom well-being.

MARCELLA'S DEFENCE 7:

When with the cooperation of the Ottawa Police, visitation was arranged to take place at the office of a community services organization, officers in this service organization declined to participate in any other contact with the Plaintiff, thereby destroying the potential for executing any further contact with this Mother.

EDITORIAL NOTE: This is one of Marcella's greatest lies and shows her plan all along: "to destroy the potential for executing any further contact with this Mother." Having investigated the matter, it is apparent that Marcella hired Robert Griffin Jr to intimidate the Nepean, Rideau and Osgoode Community Resource Centre not to have relations with the Plaintiff any longer, after the Plaintiff revealed that they were ready to testify in court, if required, against Marcella and her father from having blocked them from being able to provide vitally needed social services support to the Plaintiff's Mother. When Robert Griffin Jr. got wind of this he revealed this to Marcella, who instructed him to visit the Centre on 15 June 2015 to "convince" them not to. Robert Griffin Jr. also visited the new residence of the Plaintiff and committed assault against the Plaintiff and illegally threatened him not to contact friends or family about the activities of Marcella or he would seek to charge the Plaintiff.

Griffin also sent threatening text messages to the Plaintiff that the Plaintiff has saved; and appeared coach Ms. Alison Timmons, who works at the Neapan, Rideau and Osgoode Community Resource Centre to make a false affidavit.

Notwithstanding this, we at The Canadian note that there are plenty of other locations that Marcella could have enabled access to the Plaintiff's Mom but chose not to. This included an offer by a local Ottawa Catholic Church in early July 2015 that Marcella ignored. The Plaintiff's lawyer contacted Marcella in a letter dated 7 July 2015 to initiate the Offer at this alternative facility.

REPLY 7.

After the Plaintiff met with his Mother on 12 June 2015, the Defendants sought to block further access by apparently instructing Robert Griffin Jr, to meet with representatives of the Nepean, Rideau and Osgoode Community Resource Centre on 15 June 2015 to cease further meetings. Following this meeting, the Nepean, Rideau and Osgoode Community Resource Centre issued a letter dated 15 June 2015 that the Plaintiff was not to further contact this Centre. The Defendants' Point No. 7 is propaganda.

Marcella Carby-Samuels Sued: Lund University Shows Questionable Judgement on the Ph.D. candidate – Part 2

MARCELLA'S DEFENCE 8:

The Defendant submits that the Plaintiff initiated numerous specious harassing 911 calls that speciously directed the police to the Defendant's home.

REPLY 8.

At least one of the 911 calls initiated by the Plaintiff was credited to the Plaintiff's Mom as having saved her life before the Plaintiff had been evicted against the wishes of his Mom. The 911 calls were made out of safety concerns for the Plaintiff's Mom based upon reports made by neighbours to the Plaintiff that Horace Carby-Samuels continued to neglect the Plaintiff's Mom.

When the Plaintiff finally saw his Mom having lost the ability to speak and write and smelling like fecal matter, it is apparent that these 911 calls were very justified based upon 'before' and 'after' photographic evidence.

MARCELLA'S [and her father's] DEFENCE 9:

For a while the Plaintiff had stopped the numerous calls and harassment, however, he appears not to have found himself another way to carry on the 'harassment' by filing a vexatious legal action.

REPLY 9.

The Defendant's use of the term "harassment" is simply a code word for attempts by the Plaintiff to contact his Mom and to protect her from a pattern of abuse and neglect that the Defendant has subjected the Plaintiff and his Mom.

MARCELLA'S [and her father's] DEFENCE 10:

Further, the defendant pleads that the Plaintiff went so far as to attend to court and swear a declaration which claimed that the Defendant Horace Carby-Samuels was insane; thereby compelling the police to take the Defendant to be medically tested at the hospital late one night.

EDITORIAL NOTE: At least one witness complained that Horace kept ranting about "demons" and other witnesses complained of hostile and violent interactions that appeared to be irrational behaviour.

One neighbour who visited 30, Jarlan Terrace had complained to the Plaintiff that he saw his Mom half-naked and apparently without any good food in the house. Police had interviewed her before they medically got Horace checked at the hospital as further endorsed by a Justice of the Police who had examined evidence that the Plaintiff had presented her Honour.

REPLY 10.

A medical examination of Horace Carby-Samuels, was initiated, based upon due diligence by both the Justice of the Peace and the Ottawa Police who contacted neighbours to establish whether there were grounds for a medical examination and was also made in conjunction with consultation with officers of the Ontario government. There was no such swearing that Horace Carby-Samuels was "insane" as alleged by the Defendants.

MARCELLA'S [and her father's] DEFENCE 11:

The Defendants state that they have not prevented the Plaintiff from seeing his severely incapacitated mother and visitation encounters with his mother could be arranged, however, only under terms of adequate safety and supervision, having regard to his efforts/threats to capture or kidnap her.

EDITORIAL NOTE: We, at The Canadian, have obtained, a copy of yet another Legal Demand Letter issued by the Plaintiff's lawyer before Christmas that Marcella along with her father did not respond to. This is another apparent lie orchestrated by Marcella, who has prevented Raymond from seeing his Mother against the wishes of both him and his Mother. Marcella had simply wanted the Plaintiff "out of the way" and not caring for his Mother, who, he sought to take care of and who had been successfully helping with her recovery.

REPLY 11.

The Defendants alleged that they have not prevented the Plaintiff from seeing his Mother while at the same time complaining to police that attempts made by the Plaintiff to see his Mom constitute "harassment" while getting the Centre that had begun to initiate meetings to stop doing so by getting Robert Griffin Jr., to interfere in the work of the Nepean, Rideau and the Osgoode Resource Centre was doing on behalf of the Plaintiff and his Mom.

Mr. Griffin is an apparent "rogue" cop that the Defendants privately recruited to engage in illicit activities against the rights of the Plaintiff. This rogue cop physically threatened the Plaintiff on more than one occasion and also illegally demanded that the Plaintiff stop contacting relatives upon the direction of Marcella Carby-Samuels and not the Plaintiff's relatives he had admitted.

The Ottawa Police had delegated the Nepean, Rideau and Osgoode Resource Centre to enable contact between the Plaintiff and his Mom, and the Defendants then used the rogue cop services of Dr. Griffin to unravel the coordination secured by the Ottawa Police to obtain the services of this Centre.

Furthermore, the Defendants ignored a Legal Demand Letter in July 2015 sent to encourage the Defendants to facilitate access between the Plaintiff and his Mom.

[Appendix 2] *; and that letter was ignored just like the most recent letter written by the Plaintiff to the Defendants' Legal Representative dated 16 December 2015

[Appendix 3]*.

MARCELLA'S [and her father's] DEFENCE 12:

The defendants also plead it is the Plaintiff who is harassing and malicious with his intent to destroy his sister and her professional career.

REPLY 12.

Marcella Carby-Samuels lied to the Police in the initial report that she made on 8 January 2015 (15-5493) against the Plaintiff, and in subsequent reports and has spearheaded an apparent campaign the criminalize the Plaintiff that would lead to the eviction of the Plaintiff from his home.

The legal efforts of the Plaintiff to clear his name from the lies of the Defendants are "destroying his sister and her professional career".

Marcella is a sister of the Plaintiff in name only. In practice, Marcella is a liar who has sought to criminalize the Plaintiff and destroy her Mother without empathy or integrity.

MARCELLA'S [and her father's] DEFENCE 13:

Additionally, the Defendant Horace Carby-Samuels states the Plaintiff is fabricating reports about his sister's lobbying to get out of his parents' will.

EDITORIAL NOTE: While she could still talk, when the Plaintiff was still being the active caregiver, the Plaintiff's Mom while shaking, informed the Plaintiff of the activities that the Defendants had been planning and informed him that Marcella was also "sucking up" to her father to manipulate him. The Plaintiff's Mom said that she told her husband that Raymond is her only son which was a comment ignored by the Defendants who had shown no integrity toward the Plaintiff and his Mother.

REPLY 13.

It is the Defendants who fabricate and machinate against the Plaintiff.

---

* Please note that Appendices are in the original documents filed with the Court against Marcella and her father's actions.

MARCELLA'S [and her father's] DEFENCE 14:

The Defendant Horace Carby-Samuels states the Plaintiff's claim about contributing to the operation of the household up to over $1,000.00 per is essentially not true and again a fallacy.

EDITORIAL NOTE: Raymond has also spent thousands of dollars associated with court costs in trying to see his Mom who he as not seen since 12 June 2015 thanks to the illicit and illegal activities of the Defendants and their hired helper Robert Griffin. If you are as outraged by the activities of Marcella, who has been working both for Lund University and the United Nations while blocking the Plaintiff and his Mom seeing each other into Christmas Day. You can donate via PayPal by contacting us via Agorapublishing.com and we would then forward these donations to the Legal Defence of the Plaintiff.

REPLY 14.

The Plaintiff would not be able to afford to rent and furnish his current place and buy food among other expenses incurred as a result of the Defendants demonstrated lack of empathy to the Plaintiff if he was not in a financial position to contribute over $1,000 per month to expenses at 30 Jarlan Terrace.

If we believe the Defendant's story that this was not possible, the Plaintiff should have been living on the streets after he was evicted because "after all" according to the Defendants, the Plaintiff was a "freeloader" without the money to support household expenses that he had provided.

MARCELLA'S DEFENCE 15:

Robert Griffin [is] a detective in the elder abuse unit of the Ottawa City Police who was assigned to see that the Plaintiff desisted in his continuing harassment of the Defendants; he was also assigned to assist our accommodation to the new living arrangements ad the Plaintiff's assertion about the function of Mr. Griffin as a personal agent also demonstrates another fallacy.

REPLY 15

Robert Griffin pursued apparent illicit activities against the Plaintiff on behalf of the Defendants. He would show-up outside of his normal working hours and never once showed his police badge and appeared to be working on behalf of the Defendants in a clandestine arrangement consistent with a "rogue" or "dirty cop".

MARCELLA'S [and her father's] DEFENCE 16:

The Defendant states that the allegation made to the effect that Horace Carby-Samuels attacked and assaulted the Plaintiff causing bodily harm in another fabrication to this narrative concocted in the Plaintiff's mind as the Plaintiff injured himself by acting stupidly, but subsequent to that event, and his report of the event to the police, he formulated the imputation of an attack by Horace Carby-Samuels.

EDITORIAL NOTE: One evening the Plaintiff was standing beside the refrigerator in the kitchen when he began to express concern about the continuing neglect of the Plaintiff's Mother.

The Plaintiff tells us at The Canadian that within seconds, Horace developed a wild-eyed angry stare, began shouting and charged Plaintiff who was standing beside the refrigerator. He then took out a sharp knife out of the kitchen drawer beside the refrigerator and pointed it toward the defendant's stomach within less than a centimetre.

The Plaintiff immediately grabbed the knife with his left hand to prevent from being stabbed in the stomach by the Plaintiff resulting in an almost severed "pinkie" finger and critical nerve that required emergency reconstructive surgery and about six months of physical rehabilitation. The initial police report did not contain the full details of the incident in order to spare Marcella's father from a possible jail sentence, and also since the Plaintiff was living at 30 Jarlan Terrace; but this report was later amended when the Plaintiff lived at his current address and was safely away from Marcella's and Horace's violence.

Horace took violence against Marcella's violence against the Plaintiff by offering to do favours that including buying new fixtures in bathrooms at 30 Jarlan Terrace in exchange for Marcella getting her father's loyalty ignoring all physical and psychological violence perpetuated against the Plaintiff.

Marcella would ignore the violence that her father perpetrated against the Plaintiff's Mom and Horace would ignore the violence he also sought to perpetrate against the Plaintiff in an alleged criminal conspiracy.

REPLY 16.

Horace Carby-Samuels inflicted bodily assault against the Plaintiff that is consistent with the Plaintiff's Mom's handwritten note of abuse and is consistent with reports that persons with Type 2 Diabetes can have violent tendencies as a result of their diabetic state.

If Horace was not the perpetrator of an attack against the Plaintiff, then why did Horace not make the call to 911 having alleged that the Plaintiff cut himself? It was the Plaintiff who made the call to 911.

Horace did not call 911 because he was the attacker. Ottawa Police officers would accept the amended Police Report filed by the Plaintiff against Horace Carby-Samuels because the Plaintiff's representation of the facts was consistent with the forensic evidence. The wound experienced by The Plaintiff could not have been self-inflicted.

MARCELLA'S [and her father's] DEFENCE 17:

At no time did the Defendant Horace Carby-Samuels prevent Raymond from carting away his personal effects. When, with the supervision and assistance of The Ottawa Police, he was allowed to recover his personal effects and belongings, he cherry-picked the material and left the bulk of his belongings on the premises at 30 Jarlan Terrace. However, the material was moved to U Haul storage, (and then transferred to him) thereby by allowing him to use his non-removal of the material, as legal leverage to regain entry to the premises.

EDITORIAL NOTE: The Defendants apparently mean that they did not want the Plaintiff to be able to see his Mom, and feared that the property that they were denying access to the Plaintiff could be used as a legal means for the Plaintiff being able to see his Mom on site who was beginning to get less and less mobile thanks to the activities of the Defendants. It is apparent that the eviction perpetuated by the Defendants was illegal – and made with the support of Marcella's operative Robert Griffin – because such an eviction would have required the consent of both Horace Carby-Samuels and the Plaintiff's Mom's endorsement as a co-owner of 30, Jarlan Terrace.

In the illegal eviction perpetuated by the Defendants, Marcella used her operative Robert Griffin to deny her request to at least see her son on weekends.

REPLY 17.

Horace Carby-Samuels only released the majority of the Plaintiff's belongings after a Demand Letter from the Plaintiff's Lawyer, and the reason he elected to do this is that Horace had stopped allowing the Plaintiff on Jarlan Terrance and declared to the Ottawa Police that 30, Jarlan Terrace would be "off-limits" to the Plaintiff. The idea that the

Plaintiff voluntarily "cherry-picked" his belongings and left them at 30, Jarlan Terrance is another lie.

Furthermore, Horace did not give the entire personal belongings back to the Plaintiff which is a part of the Plaintiff's Statement of Claim.

MARCELLA'S [and her father's] DEFENCE 18:

The Defendants state that the appendix purporting to be a set of written statements by the Plaintiff's mother is in all likelihood a forgery, in light of the mother's writing incapacity.

REPLY 18.

The allegation by the Defendants that attached notes associated with the Plaintiff's Statement of Claim are forgeries, are slanderous.

At the time when the Horace with the backing of Marcella evicted the Plaintiff, Dezrin could still walk and write under the care of the Plaintiff that Marcella sought to remove from 30, Jarlan Terrace to apparently expedite the decline in the health of the Plaintiff's Mom while also seeking to eliminate the Plaintiff's Mom as a witness to the lies of the Defendants.

MARCELLA'S [and her father's] DEFENCE 19:

The Defendants hereby ask the court to review the Plaintiff's claim and dismiss said claim as it does not disclose a reasonable cause of action.

REPLY 19.

The Defendants' opposition to the said Claim is based upon verifiable lies and slander and appears to lack any supporting affidavit submitted within the time required to file a defence. Therefore, the Defendants have not presented a bona fide statement of Defence. The Plaintiff asks that the Statement of Defence is declared as invalid by the Court and for the Court to proceed with Summary Judgment against the Defendants who have sought to mislead the Court.

OVERALL:

The Defendants who in their Statement of Defence, admit to the severe physical incapacity of the Plaintiff's Mom, who they continue to deny the ability to see her son – contrary to their laughable pretence of doing otherwise – betray their total lack of morality, and specifically their lack of human decency they have demonstrated and continue to perpetuate against the Plaintiff and his Mom.

[Original Signed by the Plaintiff]

Has Marcella skilfully manipulated her father who is a co-defendant in an apparent agenda to condemn the Plaintiff's Mom to a "slow death". Has Marcella committed a terrible atrocity against the Plaintiff and his Mother?

You, be the judge!

Marcella Lying-Sister: Lund University, Ph.D. Candidate Hires Cop to Pursue Illegal Activities against Mom and Brother

When an elderly person dies in the community, a whole library burns down with him or her" is a popular saying in Africa, but that has been contrasted by recent happenings between a daughter and her father on one side and a son and the mother on another side. If care is not taken, a time will come when the elderly in society will feel very scared of living and even the mere thought of getting old will become a nightmare for all people. In a society where women are seen as being more caring and loving, it is quite unbelievable to know that a daughter, and for that matter a woman, has been able to subject her mother and brother to a very painful life on earth. Well, this act of injustice will be very hard to commit for a lot of people, but that isn't the case with Marcella Carby-Samuels, Lund University, Ph.D. Candidate, who also happens to be the daughter of Dezrin – the mother at the receiving end of all this wickedness.

Something that started as a small family issue that could be settled easily with little effort has escalated into something very sinister and scary with the mother's life at stake. It all started when Marcella left home to live in another country, leaving her mom, brother, and father at home. Daily abuses of the mother by their father led to the son, Raymond Samuels II, trying everything possible to get the mother all the care and support that she needs. To Raymond's surprise, her sister just switched on her demonic personality and joined their father in slowly and agonizingly killing their mom.

Family feuds are very common occurrences, but none of them has seen a daughter going to the extent of hiring someone to help them with the dirty acts. That is how far Marcella was willing to go by hiring a Cop named Robert Griffin Jr, who works with the Ottawa Police Department, to intimidate people who have decided to help her mother gain some freedom and the much needed medical attention that she required. The illegal activities of Robert came to light when Raymond learned that the Nepean, Rideau and Osgoode Community Resource Centre had changed their mind on assisting him to get support and justice for his mom barely three days after the same institution assured him of their total support for him.

No institution can boast of being the perfect institution, but when the life of a human being is concerned, common sense should take precedence over egoistic stupidity. Sadly enough, Robert who was hired by Marcella threw all caution to the wind and threatened the Centre until they caved in, to the selfish demands of the daughter.

When there is love, one is always ready and willing to sacrifice everything just to make sure that the loved one is safe and secured. This is exactly what Raymond has been doing, sacrificing his all in a bid to ensure that his mom gets supported.

Even among the animals, a mother does not turn on her little ones neither does the little ones turn on their mother and so when something of this nature is allowed to go on for a very long time among humans then it is right to say that there are some irregularities with the system. All hands are therefore needed on deck to ensure that the perpetrators of this heinous crime are made to account for their evil deeds to let people know that the system still cares for every single life.

Marcella Lying-Sister: Lund University, Ph.D. Candidate Condemns Mother to Total Destruction

Top universities like Lund University in Sweden try to ensure that their Ph.D. candidates are of good character, but one of their candidates, Canadian-born Marcella Carby-Samuels, is a major player in a case of domestic abuse and neglect involving an elderly invalid who happens to be her mother.

Mom gets better – daughter furious

The family dispute which came to a head in June 2015 coincided with a marked improvement in Mrs. Carby-Samuels' physical condition. This had been achieved through the dedicated care of Marcella Carby-Samuels' brother, Raymond Carby-Samuels. As a result of improvements in her health brought about by good medical care and a healthy diet, Marcella Carby-Samuels' mother had improved mobility and was even able to perform some basic household tasks that she had not been able to perform before.

But instead of being thankful for the obvious improvements in her mother's health, Marcella Carby-Samuels became 'enraged'. Despite evidence of abuse and neglect of her mother on the part of her father, Marcella Carby-Samuels conspired with him to have her brother excluded from access to his mother.

Since the elderly Mrs. Carby-Samuels had low mobility, this was achieved through excluding him from the family home. At all times, Mrs. Carby-Samuels had expressed the desire to have access to her son, but both her daughter and her husband continue to prevent the two from meeting each other.

Rapid deterioration without proper care

Deprived of her caregiver, the invalid's condition deteriorated from June 2015 onwards, and in a very short time, she was no longer able to walk at all and became unable to speak. Alarmed by the evidence of his mother's deterioration in health and physical appearance, Raymond Carby-Samuels called upon social services to intervene, but after a few visits, social workers were also denied access to Mrs. Carby-Samuels.

Although aware of the ongoing decline in her mother's health, Marcella Carby-Samuels continued to turn a blind eye to the evidence of neglect and abuse observed by her brother, continuing to side with her father – a man who was known to be neglectful of his wife's physical needs. When Raymond Carby-Samuels still had access to his mother, he would often return from work to find that she had not even been provided with food and water during the day.

There are even indications of physical abuse. During the dispute leading up to Raymond Carby-Samuels' banning from the family home, Mr. Carby-Samuels Sr., struck his wife, and a desperate, written attempt on the part of the invalid to report ongoing abuse was grossly mishandled by Ottawa police.

Who is the real victim?

As a result of the actions taken by Marcella Carby-Samuels, her mother has been denied access to her son, has ceased to receive proper care, is neglected, and is possibly even abused at a time of life when every Canadian citizen should be assured of the best care possible. Ironically, Marcella Carby-Samuels, who has left her mother in an unsustainable situation, will be completing her Ph.D. in Sustainable Development at Lund University.

Human Ecology: UN Consultant, Ph.D. Candidate Marcella Lying-Sister Practices Hypocrisy

A lot of studies have been carried out by renowned researchers on humans and the effects that their actions have on the environment which is referred to as "Human Ecology". In a publication by Ellen Swallow Richards, human ecology is defined as "The study of the surroundings of human beings in the effects they produce in the lives of men". This has led to the belief that all actions of humans do have either a direct or indirect impact on the lives of others. It is for a reason like this that the behaviour shown by Ph.D. Candidate Marcella Carby-Samuels should not be taken lightly at all.

Looking at the devastating effects left on Dezrin Carby-Samuels by her daughter Marcella Carby-Samuels and husband Horace Carby-Samuels, one is spot on, right to conclude that such actions by the daughter and her father are hypocrisy of the highest order.

According to an article titled "Holocene Extinction", the activities of humans do have a direct or indirect bearing on the extinction of species from the surface of the earth. This can be seen in the case currently being discussed. The actions of Marcella and her father have led to Dezrin being rejected by even her Jamaican relatives and some members of the society where she lives. Her current condition is that of a sorry one.

The United Nations is an organization that is recognized for its desire to ensure that all the basic necessities of life like food, shelter, education, and health are adequately provided for both the young and old. Therefore, whoever gets the opportunity to work for the UN is always regarded as having greater respect and love for human life. This is why it is very worrying as Marcella Carby-Samuels, who once worked as a Consultant at the UN, has shown behaviour that contradicts the aims and visions of the UN. This begs the question, "How can someone who works for the UN amid all their advocacies for the survival of humans, especially the aged be so mean and heartless to her mother? This clearly shows that Marcella Carby-Samuels is an individual who practices pure hypocrisy.

Although the UN has been for a very long time now advocating for human rights all over the world, it has also added the human rights of older persons to their aims and objectives. This was after it concluded that the elderly in society were having their rights trampled upon. Four main aspects were highlighted and they are; discrimination, poverty, violence, and abuse. A lot of other organizations have also joined forces with the UN in helping to ensure that the elderly are well catered for in the societies that they live.

With all that the UN is doing for the elderly in the communities, it is very serious to find out that their Consultant had not only discriminated against her aged mother, but also condoned the violence and abuse meted to her mother by her father. If not a hypocrite, who else in his or her right senses and as a human would even secretly wish for his or her mother to be in such a condition of absolute helplessness?

UN Scandal Erupts: Marcella Carby-Samuels Oppresses Voiceless Elderly Mom

The fact that the United Nations has been one of the vibrant organizations that fights for the rights of people is not a new thing. This is an organization that since its establishment, fought for people, especially children and the elderly in societies to be accorded some degree of freedom and protection. Through the various humanitarian activities of the United Nations, billions of people who were once oppressed are now free. It is therefore very surprising and equally scandalous to find out that a Ph.D. candidate who some time ago worked in the capacity as a UN consultant has been the brain behind all the maltreatments and total neglect of an elderly woman.

The case of Dezrin Carby-Samuels being oppressed by her daughter, Marcella Carby-Samuels and her husband, Horace is one that has rocked the very core foundations of human nature and raised questions about how wicked can a person be all in a bid to satisfy his or her ego. Even if education wasn't enough to bring the desired change in Marcella, at least having worked with a humanitarian organization as notable as the UN, should have instilled in her, the love of humans. However, she has thrown away the very things that the UN preaches and practices away and resorted to carrying out her evil deeds together with her father.

For quite some time now, the main wish of Dezrin has been to be reconciled with her son, Raymond. However, this simple request of hers has been vehemently denied by her daughter and husband. This elderly woman whose health has deteriorated drastically had sought to find some love and affection from her son who has been the pillar holding her life together but that wish was never respected by Marcella and Horace.

The distinguishing feature between humans and the wildest of animals is that humans have some degree of decency when human life is involved. What makes this case a big scandal is that Marcella is a human, has also worked at the biggest humanitarian organization in the world and is now even pursuing her Ph.D. With all these attributes, it is completely unfathomable to realize that she has been one of the architects of her mother's declining health condition. The attitude and behaviour of Marcella, therefore, is a smack in the face of the United Nations as she has trampled on the very core values that the organization cherishes.

If a daughter can commit such atrocities against her mother then the survival of the human race is at risk unless something is done and very fast.

UN Scandal: Marcella Carby-Samuels Presents Lies to Ottawa Court

UN employees and consultants are generally expected to have unimpeachable reputations, but one of their consultants, Marcella Carby-Samuels, has demonstrated evidence that she is a pathological liar in her testimony related to the Claim No:15-SC-138297 presented an Ontario Court in Ottawa. Has Marcella Carby-Samuels become a compulsive or pathological liar in her efforts to subvert her own Mom's and brother's rights? You, be the judge!

"This is not my address"

Carby-Samuels claims that Jarlan Terrace, the address at which she apparently receives mail from active Canadian bank accounts, and where much of her belongings are kept, is not her address and that she was not served properly, in the claim by her brother, Raymond. In her objection, she insisted that, Jarlan Terrace had not been her address for 20 years or more. Yet, when required to state her address in a subsequent motion, she gave her address as Jarlan Terrace.

To the most impartial observer, this would seem remarkable. The address which she claims is 'not hers', suddenly becomes her address. Logically, she is either lying about Jaraln Terrace being her address or lying about it not being her address.

Which is true? Her bank would certainly assert that, Jarlan Terrace is, indeed, her address.

"He is not a lawyer"

In further objections, Ms. Carby-Samuels stated that Mr. Ji, her brother's lawyer, was "only a law student" and not a fully practicing lawyer. However, the law society of Upper Canada confirms that Mr. Ji has been a practicing lawyer since 2014. One is inclined to wonder what the next lie to be presented to the court will be.

"This is not my mother"

Although Ms. Carby-Samuels has not made this particular claim, the background to the case which is being heard by the Ontario court in Ottawa is deeply shocking.

Carby-Samuels' brother is bringing the claim against her owing to her complicity in the neglect of their elderly mother.

This situation has led to a rapid decline in her physical health, to the point where she is no longer able to communicate or walk.

Carby-Samuels' brother, had previously been caring for their mother, but she has supported her father in his determined efforts to ensure that mother and son should not have access to one another. Social workers have confirmed that the elderly

Mrs. Carby-Samuels had expressed the wish to have access to her son. But as an invalid, she is unable to leave the family home from which her son has been barred through a conspiracy between Marcella Carby-Samuels and her father. After this action, neglect and mistreatment have led to Mrs. Carby-Samuels' decline.

———— ✥ ————

Lund University's Marcella Carby-Samuels: Mind of a Psychopath Betrays Mom

Psychopaths have always been seen as hardcore criminals who can easily be identified even by their physical appearance. However, a close look at CBC's- Doc Zone, on YouTube presents a whole new dimension to who can be classified as a psychopath.

Even with the most dangerous and hardened criminals and dictators of all time, not a single one of them will be able to perpetuate the kind of apparent evil that a Ph.D. candidate at Lund University by name Marcella Carby-Samuels has been able to do. At least as with most criminals, their evil acts are always committed against people outside their family circle and it is for this reason that Marcella Carby-Samuels' evil deeds against her mother defy all known human cruelties.

When one takes his or her time to watch CBC's video on YouTube about psychopaths and who qualifies to be referred as such, one will be hit with the hard truth that psychopaths are not always criminal by looks as some of them can take the form of a very charming and seemingly friendly human being. However, this is only a public relations facade to help in their quest to unleash all kinds of evil and havoc on their innocent and helpless victims without ever being suspected by the majority of people. This is just a true description of Marcella Carby-Samuels, who has defied all human empathy laws and treated her mother in the most despicable way that can ever be imagined.

She was able to even convince professionally trained police officers to side with her in preventing her brother, Raymond, from seeing their mother, Dezrin. Psychopaths have been described as lacking empathy and always driven by their insatiable quest to acquire money and power. In Marcella's case, she has been aware of her mother's wish to see her son, Raymond, but that has been blatantly refused by Marcella and the last time that Dezrin saw her son was on the 12th of June 2015.

Dezrin had for a very long time been subjected to all kinds of inhumane treatments from her husband, Horace Carby-Samuels and her source of hope and joy was her son. However, Marcella was able to use her charm and innocent-looking appearance to deceive the police into barring Raymond from ever visiting their mom. Marcella decided to side with her abusive father who was the genesis of all the maltreatments in his quest to obtain absolute control of the family.

Dezrin who is now left in a condition where she cannot speak, talk or walk, has always desired to see her son, but that has also been coldly ignored and denied by Marcella even to the extent of using the services of some very dirty cops in Ottawa, Canada to somehow give some legal backing to her evil deeds. Respect for the elderly in society and human empathy are the two most important things that can never be found in the dictionary of Marcella Carby-Samuels as she continues to ignore the wishes of her mother.

Editorial comment

The apparent manipulative alien replication of Horace Carby-Samuels became apparent when his signature that he has had for over 75 years all of a sudden changed in court documents. Handwriting experts asserted that the signatures of the "old Horace" and the apparent "New Horace" as a result of the "Mandela Effect" could not be from the same people. When this was revealed in Court, the judges who all had ties to the University of Ottawa all covered up this apparent anomaly. This notably includes Justice Sylvia Corthon who appeared to be very much a part of this manipulative alien orchestration against Raymond and Dezrin Carby-Samuels' plight against profound injustices.

Canada's Shame: Horace Carby-Samuels Blocks Visitation Access to Sick Elderly Wife

As Canadians, we are among the most socially progressive people when it comes to helping our fellow human beings abroad through government refugee policies and opening our homes to these refugees.

But, when it comes to rallying behind fellow human beings in Canada who are being subjected to human rights abuses at home that could involve someone in our city or our neighbourhood, we, as Canadians, may be among the least progressive among western industrialized societies.

Take, for example, the case of an elderly woman in Ottawa, Canada. Her husband has blocked visitation access to her son and police services for more than a year.

Please watch the above video. But, how many reporters outside The Canadian have been willing to provide any coverage of this human rights atrocity? The answer is "zero". How many of her friends and relatives having been made aware of how this woman has been made to essentially be a prisoner in her own home – losing her ability to talk, walk and write at the hands of her abuser has sought to come to her assistance. Thus far, zero aside from her son. Her long-time friends of more than 20 years and even her brother who lives in Toronto abandoned her because they "don't want to get involved". These are the same friends and family who this elderly Mom selflessly helped when she was able-bodied.

It is this kind of hypocrisy among Canadians that has perpetuated the abuse and battery of the elderly and other women as victims of controlling spouses like ex-Notre Dame University professor Horace Carby-Samuels. It is this kind of hypocrisy that is behind the atrocious Third World like poverty of many First Nations reserves and the homeless people who grow in numbers in our cities, in the face of Canadians at the same time opening their door to the plight of refugees.

I guess the Canadian media is too busy presenting Canada as a paradise of human rights and social justice to be bothered to provide much better coverage on human rights abuses at home that is symbolized by the kind of abusive conduct that has been perpetuated by Horace Carby-Samuels in an affluent suburb of Ottawa.

Behind those affluent doors in Ottawa and other Canadian cities, there are atrocious abuses taking place against both women and children alike that Canadian media organizations, and Canadians in general alike, seem unwilling to face and redress as compared to the "refugee problem". It is apparent that elderly women are at the bottom of Canada's socio-political "totem pole".

This elderly woman wrote notes when she could write that she was being abused.

One note reads - "**Dad abuses me.**".

Her cries to the Ottawa Police Services were simply ignored.

Horace Carby-Samuels diabolically blocked her son from defending her rights by lying to the police that her son suffered from "mental illness" that made him violent. This was a complete fabrication designed to ensure that the Ottawa Police Service would not listen to the son's representation concerning the abuse of his Mom that has now continued for more than a year.

Raymond, who is shown in the video, has not seen his Mom since 12 June 2015 -- more than a year ago! His Mom has been made a "prisoner in her own home" by her able-bodied husband who aside from mental and physical abuse had years ago seized control of money, for vexatious litigation in the Federal Court that her deceased mother in Jamaica had left for her. Horace also had blocked an Ottawa Hospital from providing her speech therapy support. As a result, Raymond's Mom lost the ability to speak. The verifiable evidence of Horace's abuse of rights and neglect is contained in litigation brought by Raymond against his Mom's husband under Court File - 15-66772.

John E Summers, is the lawyer for Horace Carby-Samuels, who has continued to enable his client to disobey a Court Order rendered by Justice Patrick Smith that sought to enable Raymond to have daily access to provide the care-giving and support he had been providing his Mom before the public mischief of Horace to the Ottawa Police Services.

Help spread social awareness by distributing the above video to your Facebook,

Twitter, and other social media pages. You're also invited to donate via PayPal in support of a legal defence fund to help liberate Raymond's Mom from being an apparent prisoner in her own home.

Petition: Day 531 – Ottawa's Horace Carby-Samuels Proves Disabled Women Can Be Kidnapped or Tortured

Today, 28 November 2016 marks the 531st day that Horace Carby-Samuels had held Dezrin, his wife, hostage in Kanata.

Dezrin Carby-Samuels' liberty has been taken away from her by her abusive husband, since 12 June 2015.

Since that time, Horace has blocked visitation access by Raymond her son, who Dezrin has sought to see, and others.

In Canada, we are used to the idea that we have a Canadian Charter of Rights and Freedoms that protects us all.

But, this is not the case. Horace, once and for all, proves that this is little more than an illusion for many disabled people and other Canadians.

Horace proves that if you're a woman, and you had the bad luck of being subjected to spousal abuse, your husband can bind and gag you to a chair in your own home, and there's literally nothing that the police can do if they don't hear you screaming, if they even receive a judicial order by our son to enable access.

Horace Carby-Samuels for now 531 DAYS has kept his wife locked up in their Kanata home!

When Ottawa police visited 30, Jarlan Terrace in Kanata with the support of a Judicial Order issued by Justice Patrick Smith, Horace just refused these cops any access. (VIDEO above)

Horace then hired a sleazy lawyer named John Summers to "set aside" the order as Horace continued to subject his wife to abuse and neglect.

Thanks to Horace's actions, Dezrin can no longer walk, write and talk. The efforts of Raymond, Dezrin's son, to spare his Mom from an abusive husband gone wild has been undermined by a Canadian system that apparently can be easily manipulated by abusers.

So, you see ladies, you won the right to vote, but you don't have as much equality as you think.

Men still rule, and even if you co-own your home, cops will view YOUR home to be your male partner's possession, and if your male partner has you tied up and in the basement in a dungeon of Hell, and you can't scream, don't expect that cops will be able to save you if your husband doesn't want those cops on "HIS" property.

Horace once referred to 'integrity' as the most important human characteristic.

It is therefore somewhat ironic that Horace has prevented Dezrin, his wife, seeing her own son through the use of lies.

Among Horace's lies, has been that Raymond, his son, "suffers from mental illness".

He then got John Summers, a sleazy lawyer from Bell Baker to embellish Horace's lies by preparing a fraudulent affidavit.

Petition: Day 513 – Ottawa's Horace Carby-Samuels Puts Disabled Wife Through Living Hell

Here, at *The Canadian*, we're covering the on-going horrific oppression of the human rights of Dezrin Carby-Samuels in her Ottawa home. It is important to consider just what kind of Hell this poor woman has been subjected to. Think, for a moment, you not being able to walk, write or talk for more than 500 days. For most of us, that would be Hell enough. But, for Dezrin Carby-Samuels the hell created for her by Horace her own husband, and Marcella her very own daughter is even worse.

Let's just imagine that you had been slaving for over 50 years to cook, clean and go everything you possibly could do for your significant other. You ever quit your career. Add to that you have literally saved the life of your significant other more than once.

Imagine yourself 5'0 tall and just over 100 lbs compared to your significant other who is 6'4" and nearly 200 lbs with a large build having been a former athlete.

Then imagine you developing an illness that with the proper treatment and the right balance of nutrition could be managed or even cured. Now imagine that just when you learned of this ailment you became the target of psychological abuse which morphed into physical abuse by the partner that you had been supporting emotionally and economically for more than 50 years.

Now imagine your son stepping up to the plate by ensuring your access to medical services and even doing grocery shopping and then cooking for you as your husband further neglected you. Then imagine your husband getting jealous that your son was helping you manifesting in your husband attacking your son with a kitchen knife almost severing off one of his fingers.

Then imagine that your jealous husband plotting to get rid of your son by calling and lying to the police that your son suffers from "mental illness" which made him, your son, violent and that he has held him and you "hostage" resulting in the police evicting your son from the premises, and you never seeing your son again – or at least for more than 500 days.

Then imagine that with your son now evicted, your husband accelerated his torture and neglect of you resulting in you totally losing your ability to walk, write and talk. You are now the captive of an abuser.

A doctor recommends you get weekly speech therapy to save your voice, but your husband, whom you have done everything for, blocks it! No speech therapy for you!

Then imagine that your husband hires a dirty cop like Detective Robert Griffin to ensure that your son is threatened not to try to visit you. You hear your son trying to call and reach you, but you can't run to the door, you can't scream, and you can't sneak notes to anyone.

You're now the prisoner of an abuser, who screams at you morning, night and day -- Telling you how worthless you are. As you get sicker, he ridicules you and even physically abuses you. When you're hungry and becoming thin from a lack of food, your significant other cooks for himself eats and watches TV downstairs - totally oblivious to your needs upstairs. You only see him when he remembers you to shout, scream and further ridicule you.

Social services come to your door several times, but like your son, they too are blocked by your significant other / husband.

Conditions around you start to become unsanitary because after all, it was you and not your husband who kept things clean.

For days and weeks, you are without any proper access to the food you need to reverse your condition. Your only access to food consists of little more than potato chips and other junk food.

You want to cook for yourself, but can't. You are either ignored or attacked where you live. Your health worsens. Your spouse instead of showing the love and empathy of a husband, ridicules and screams at you.

You want to take a shower, but your husband's interest in you is for little more than abuse. Soon you begin to smell of feces since you have become immobilized.

Your daughter rather than trying to help you as your son sees this as an opportunity to send you to an early grave so she can seize control of assets. Your daughter decides to support her father's abuse of her mother so that her father will sign over the family will in her name only.

Your daughter makes up stories to embellish the lies of her father and presides over you as a co-abuser simply to ensure that she gets the control of family assets.

Your own brother, sister and the rest of your extended family and friends either don't want to get "involved" because they don't care or are apparently too scared of your husband and threats by his dirty cop to get involved.

You have been deserted by everyone except your son and social service personnel that have been blocked in getting you the support that you need.

Finally, you hear your son at the door after nearly one year who has a court order to get you the support that you need. He is with the "regular police" rather than the dirty cop that your husband has been using. However, your husband refuses both their access. You are powerless, to scream for help the police would need to enter the premises.

This is the kind of Hell that Dezrin Carby-Samuels had been living under for more than 500 days!

The video above shows Raymond attempting to visit his Mom at 30 Jarlan Terrace in Ottawa, with the support of a Court Order.

Petition: Day 512 -- Abusive Husband Holds Ottawa Woman Hostage

Today, November 8th, marks the 512th day that Dezrin Carby-Samuels had been held hostage by Horace her husband. Dezrin had written a note back in Spring 2015, that she was being abused. When the Ottawa Police visited her place of residence on 30 Jarlan Terrace, they simply ignored her note, You might ask why? Horace coordinated the ignoring of evidence by a dirty copy working within the police whose name is Detective Robert Griffin Jr.. Thanks to Horace and this dirty cop, Dezrin has not been able to see Raymond, her son, and other people.

Horace, who is an ex-federal civil servant, has been blocking visitation access that Dezrin has sought since 12 June 2015. Thanks to the abuse that Dezrin has suffered, she is no longer able to walk, write or talk. When Raymond was taking care of his Mom up until the end of April 2015, Dezrin was an able-bodied woman who sought to protect his Mom from Horace's abuse. But back in April, Horace co-ordinated a lie with Robert Griffin that Raymond "suffers from a mental illness" and a basis of evicting him from taking care of his Mom.

Without the protection of Raymond, Dezrin suffered abuse and neglect from her husband that has continued now for 512 days! Horace even ignored Justice Patrick's Smith's Order dated 11 February 2016 which demanded that Horace enable access. Horace hired John Summers who then hired a corrupt Judge name Justice P. E. Roger to reverse Justice Patrick's Simth's original order.

Justice P E. Roger ignored all evidence of abuse inflicted by Horace and then fined Raymond $1500.00 for having sought access to seeing his Mom that his Mom had been requesting since Spring 2015!

The above video was taken at 30 Jarlan Terrace in Kanata, Ontario with the consent of the Ottawa Police officers who arrived there to enforce Justice Patrick Smith's Order. You will see Horace barely opening his door to these police officers who were refused access to seeing Dezrin.

The police officers could not enter the premise unless they could ascertain immediate danger. Unfortunately, Dezrin having been abused and neglected for months had lost the ability to walk, talk or write. So, when she heard the police, it would have been impossible for her to either cry out to them or run to the door.

Dezrin had become a prisoner in her own home. Across Canada, including provincial jurisdictions like British Columbia, blocked visitation access of the elderly constitutes abuse.

In this article, we, at The Canadian, have posted a photo of what Dezrin looked like when Raymond had been looking after his Mom, and what she looked like within a few weeks of being subjected to abuse and neglect, thanks to the macabre activities of Horace Carby-Samuels and his operatives.

CHAPTER 4

Nepean, Rideau, Osgoode Community Resource Centre

Editorial comment

Nepean, Rideau, Osgoode Community Resource Centre shows us how willing humans are willing to sell out themselves and other humans to a manipulative alien agenda and the corresponding complicity of the Courts under the "Mandela Effect".

Nepean, Rideau and Osgoode Resource Centre Lies Against Sick, Disabled and Elderly Client

Scenario: an elderly, disabled woman is denied access to her son who wants to care for her. She is denied access to proper care. She is neglected and is verbally and physically abused. The authorities refuse to do anything about it.

Where is this happening? In some distant, uncivilized country? No! It's happening right here in Ottawa, Canada, and it's happening as you read this!

What can you do? Well, you can shake your head and walk away as so many others have – or you can do something about it!

This elderly lady is a real person living in Ottawa right now, and she needs strong legal representation to secure her rights:

• The right to freedom of association (she may see her son if she chooses)

• The right to dignity (proper care for her personal needs)

• The right to live in peace rather than in fear of 'unstoppable' abuser.

The authorities won't lift a finger to help her. A heartrending written report of abuse in her handwriting has been treated as an 'exaggeration'. Social services have denied her access to a lawyer. She can't walk away because she is disabled. She can't phone for help because her neglect has caused a deterioration in her condition to the point where she cannot speak.

Nepean, Rideau, and Osgoode Resource Centre: Caught on Video

Social service workers are employed to help citizens and provide them support and care when abused or mistreated. That wasn't the case in the following story about a neglected elderly woman that occurred in Ottawa, Canada.

Dezrin was craving for help when she wrote down "Dad abuses me" to her son. The son took this seriously and contacted The Nepean, Rideau & Osgoode Community Resource Centre to help his mother with her violent husband. Thanks to this Resource Centre, Dezrin continued to be subjected to neglect and abuse by her husband.

In one incident, the abusive husband attacked his son with the knife and he suffered severe injuries. Ms. Timmons completely neglected that fact and in that way, she failed to protect the helpless disabled lady. Has this Resource Centre been responsible for a death sentence? The story isn't over here; Ms. Timmons caught lying on the phone during a conversation with Dezrin's son on a video that has been airing on YouTube.

Ms. Timmons had made it very clear in the video that no advocates will be allowed at the already arranged meeting. The non-ethical, social-worker would later deny her having blocked Dezrin obtaining legal defence in a signed an affidavit (verification under oath) that The Nepean, Rideau & Osgoode Community Resource Centre didn't prevent a lawyer to attend the meeting.

It is disgraceful how Ms. Timmons managed the whole situation and her negligence, lack of morals and ethics are evident. Even though this Resource Centre and police have shockingly sided with the abusive husband are against him, Dezrin's son is still persistent in his decision to fight for his mother's constitutional rights and he will not rest before he facilitates the affirmation of his Mom's inviolable rights. The elderly and disabled woman should be protected, but the uninterested social service agency had left her unprotected.

This is not the first time social services have neglected similar cases. The discrimination and the lack of morals is regular in the system and when that happens, people are suffering. The old, and disabled people have the same rights as anyone else and the handling of this problem is simply disgraceful. A person with a disability is a person with rights.

People with disabilities can participate equally in society if we remove physical and attitudinal barriers. Ageism (discrimination against old people), in addition to racism and sexism, is the most widespread and most brutal form of discrimination in our society. Most seniors are rightly wondering why someone who spent his life creating and working, when it came time to reap the fruits of their labour, is stigmatized just because of their age?

Nepean, Rideau, and Osgoode Resource Centre Lies on Video

Social workers have a crucial role in society to make sure people's rights are not violated and that citizens of all ages, backgrounds, and social statuses are protected by means that are regulated by the law. However, even the best of systems with the most educated people will have its flaws. Unfortunately, when the system fails people will get hurt and they will quickly become victims of the system that's supposed to protect them. To make it worse, this isn't happening in a third world country. It seems as though some social workers in Canada lack the ethics and morals that are needed to protect the underprivileged, the sick, and the helpless.

Dezrin Carby-Samuels, who is a resident of Ottawa, was desperate for help and all she wanted was her son to keep being her caregiver. Despite her wishes, her violent and abusive husband managed to persuade the police and social workers to stop her son from even visiting his mother. Ms. Timmons, the social worker assigned to the case, chose to ignore the son's testimony, the husband's police record, and a heart-breaking note that the elderly mother passed off to her son in which she wrote: "Dad abuses me". All of this wasn't enough to convince the social worker that Mrs. Dezrin would be in grave danger if she was left at the mercy of her violent husband.

In one family incident that occurred, the elderly woman's husband attacked the son with a knife which resulted in severe injuries. And despite knowing all of these events, Ms. Timmons still thought it would be best if the abusive husband assumed the role of her caregiver. Sadly enough for everyone involved, this heartbreaking story isn't about to get any better. The social worker was caught lying in a phone call that the desperate son made to the Nepean, Rideau and Osgoode Resource Centre. In this phone call, she makes it clear that no lawyers will be allowed in a previously arranged meeting. Soon after she signed an affidavit in which she claimed that the Community Resource Center did not prevent a lawyer to be present.

The victim's son is adamant to keep fighting for his mother's rights, despite the police and social services working against him. When any particular system that exists for the sole purpose of defending people's rights goes this far in committing such a horrific act of negligence is when the community needs to stand up and speak out for what's right. Nothing can undo the horrors this family has gone through, but with the truth on their side, hopefully, this loving son will be reunited with his mother before her health deteriorates further.

Nepean, Rideau, and Osgoode Community Resource Centre Scandal Erupts

If you thought that the intrigue surrounding Mike Duffy, and other Conservative Party senators was the worst scandal to hit Ottawa this year that is probably because you have not heard of one involving one particular intake social worker who is affiliated with the Nepean, Rideau & Osgoode Community Resource Centre (NROCRC). These well-known scandals plastered over the local Ottawa and Canadian mainstream media involved breaches of public trust, but did not threaten human life in contrast with the apparent activities of the NROCRC.

Shortly after mid-April 2015, the NROCRC was directed to contact the son of an elderly and disabled senior citizen who has lived in Kanata. The son had been the primary caregiver of his Mom. She had been forcibly separated from her son by an abusive husband who had become jealous of the son's presence as the caregiver alongside his abuse. The son has been preparing meals and providing other support to his Mom alongside the father who became a "terror" in the house who in a rage almost severed the son's finger two years ago.

Well, Ms. Timmons was delegated with the responsibility to contact the son promptly so that the son could resume his care-giving somehow. The Mom whose name is Dezrin, had told the Ottawa Police that she had wanted to see her son no less frequently than every weekend.

Can you believe that by the time Ms. Timmons scheduled a meeting, Dezrin had lost her ability to speak and walk on her own, after being able to still do household work and look after herself while the son was looking after her? Ms. Timmons did nothing for Dezrin for many weeks, blaming her husband for blocking access. She blamed the father in a meeting that the son had with her after he had seen his Mom at their office on Merivale Road on 12 June 2015.

Ms. Timmons arranged a meeting at the offices of the NROCRC on 12 June 2015.

This was several weeks after Dezrin had asked to be able to see her son regularly.

The son cried uncontrollably during the meeting and for three days after seeing the state of his Mom who was essentially being forcibly confined by the husband. This apparent forcible confinement was being done under the apparent complicity of Ms. Timmons' negligence as an intake worker of the NROCRC.

But this is only the beginning of the scandal. In preparation for that Meeting, the son wanted to bring a lawyer to act in defence of his Mom's rights. However, Ms. Timmons told the son that she would not allow the lawyer to be present. She then lied in a written affidavit to have ever sought to block access. The video that shows the lack of integrity operating at the NROCRC has been published above. In this video, you will hear Ms. Timmons emphatically blocking access to a now sick elderly woman that was being abused and psychologically tortured by her husband.

Has Ms. Timmons no empathy? What kind of a social worker would turn a blind eye to affirming the civil rights of a sick, disabled and elderly woman? Much of Ms. Timmons affidavit is apparent fiction and fully consistent with established lies that this video exposes.

But it gets even worse. On 15 June 2015, the NROCRC acting on behalf of Dezrin's husband sent out a letter to the son indicating that he was never to contact the Centre again. Ms. Dezrin wanted to see her son, and nodded to her son when he asked his Mom if she wanted him to help make her better.

The son was told by the City of Ottawa staff that his only recourse would be a litigation. It was in response to his litigation that Ms. Timmons and the NROCRC decided that lying was the best strategy to deal with a rather defenceless position.

Unfortunately, they were unaware that their lies would be exposed by videotape.

Thanks to Ms. Timmons and the NROCRC working in concert with an abusive husband, the son has not seen his ailing mom since 12 June 2015.

The son was not even able to wish his mom a happy birthday on 21 August 2015 as he had always done every year with a jealous husband blocking access to Dezrin who could not now walk and talk thanks to negligence.

Ms. Timmons and the NROCRC show that egos in a not-for-profit organization can sacrifice and threaten human life in a manner that is far worse than the kind of scandal that involved Mike Duffy and the other Conservative senators. The NROCRC not only violates disability access rights guaranteed by Section 15 of the Canadian Charter and Rights and Freedoms in addition to disability rights under Ontario statutory laws, but also violates basic human decency that a supposed social services agency could not only turn such a blind eye against human suffering but also to lie in the process.

Nepean, Rideau, and Osgoode Community Resource Centre Perpetuates Elder, Wife Abuse

*A*n elderly Ottawa woman has become disabled owing to neglect by her husband after her son the primary caregiver was barred from the home by her husband with the support of the police.

The Nepean, Rideau & Osgoode Community Resource Centre was alerted to the situation, but have denied the woman access to a lawyer on their premises, later denying that they had done so, despite clear evidence to the contrary

A son seeks to enforce his mother's rights

After hearing disturbing reports from neighbours regarding his mother's state of health and the low level of care she was receiving, the man approached the Nepean, Rideau, Osgoode Community Resource Centre in the hope of facilitating a meeting between himself, his mother and a lawyer.

The assigned social worker, Ms. Timmons, confirmed that the man's mother, Mrs. Dezrin, had signified that she wished to see her son despite her husband's attempts to keep them apart. However, since the woman has become disabled to the point where she can no longer walk or speak, and her son continued to be barred from entering her home by her husband, special arrangements had to be made.

No legal recourse for a disabled woman

In a video recorded conversation from a speakerphone, Ms. Timmons confirms that a meeting at the community center has been arranged, but categorically refused to allow a lawyer to be present at the meeting.

At a later date, Ms. Timmons would sign an affidavit denying that she refused Ms. Dezrin access to a lawyer at the meeting. In the recorded conversation, Ms. Timmons confirms that the exclusion of a lawyer from the meeting was the decision of the Community Resource Centre rather than that of Ms. Dezrin.

Healthcare professionals recommend adequate care

Ms. Dezrin's son remains deeply concerned about the deterioration in her condition since her husband assumed the role of caregiver. It was also apparent from the recorded conversation that the center was 'unaware' of a hospital recommendation that Ms. Dezrin be referred to a center where she could receive critically needed speech therapy and other related care.

Do Canadian women have rights if they are disabled?

Mrs. Dezrin signified that she would like to see her son at least once a week. The social worker did not indicate that she perceived anything wrong with a situation in which a husband could prevent a disabled mother from having access to her son within her own home. After a meeting on the 12th of June, the Centre then issued a letter that it would not facilitate further meetings and that Mrs. Dezrin's son should no longer contact the Centre for help. In emails obtained by The Canadian, it's apparent that the Centre had been delegated by the Ottawa Police to facilitate ongoing get-together between Ms. Dezrin and her son, and that the letter issued by the Centre was an abdication of their social responsibilities to Ms. Dezrin under Ontario's disability access laws; and a corresponding breach of the Centre's supposed socially- facilitating, not-for-profit mandate advertised on their website.

Care, family access and legal recourse denied by husband – supported by the authorities

Simply put, a disabled woman is being neglected with the apparent complicity of police and social services, while her son has desperately sought to obtain adequate care for her.

Also, the woman's expressed wish to be allowed regular access to her son is being denied by her husband, the police and social services. Her son wishes to provide legal recourse to rectify the situation, but Ms. Dezrin is being denied legal assistance.

Ottawa: Nepean, Rideau, and Osgoode Community Resource Centre Lies -- Supports Abusive Husband

In Claim No 15-SC-136111 Alison Timmons presents an Affidavit that she never interfered with the ability of the son of an elderly and disabled woman to secure a lawyer for his Mom. However, if one watches and listens to the above video, it is apparent that Ms. Timmons, who represents the Nepean, Rideau and Osgoode Community Resource Centre and with the support the resource centre's lawyer committed perjury.

The son had reported abuse being inflicted by his Mom's husband against his Mom. His Mom's husband responded by frustrating the ability of her son to see his Mom. Under pressure by agents acting on behalf of the Mom's husband, the Center elected to support the Mom's husband against the desire of the Mom to see her son!

The Center has been involved in a pattern of apparent lying and this video exemplifies how Alison Timmons and her agents have knocked women's rights back to a time just over a century ago when women were treated as the chattel property of the husband. This is a practice that still goes on in many countries.

Dezrin cannot walk on her own or talk, thanks to the negligence of this Center. And Dezrin's husband has sought to treat her as "his property". The son who was evicted by Horace, Dezrin's jealous husband prevents Dezrin's son from visiting her under a trespassing threat by the Police and has denied Dezrin's human right to see her son.

The Ottawa Police has sought to ignore Dezrin's human rights and Ms. Alison Timmons has sought to lie to deny Dezrin, access to a lawyer. Ms. Timmons, who has sided with Horace has betrayed women everywhere. Mrs. Dezrin wrote that she has been abused, and Ms. Timons has essentially left Dezrin, to be forcibly confined in a home where she has been substantively neglected. Her son reported that when he saw his Mom, it was very apparent that his Mom's hygiene needs were not being met. Mrs. Dezrin has been described by her son as a very kind, loving and hardworking and super-hygienic person suffering under the super-control that is being exerted by Horace.

Ottawa Police, Nepean, Rideau, and Osgoode Resource Centre Abuse Elderly Woman's Rights

A Call to Action to Stop the Abuse of a Disabled Woman

When Dezrin (Carby-Samuels) was a young woman she helped others in her community through her job as a registered nurse and her thoughtfulness and kindness toward others. This wonderful mother never faltered in her commitment to her community and her family. Now, Dezrin is in poor health having lost the ability to walk and speak. It is the hope of those who care about Dezrin that the community she once cared for, that those with a passion for justice and that those with any compassion in their hearts at all will reach out to help her in her time of desperate need.

Mrs. Dezrin communicates with her son by way of written messages. One such message asked for his help. It seems Dezrin's husband has been neglectful and abusive and has even barred her, with some backing of the law, from seeing her son. This is even though this loving woman has written requesting help and a visit from the son she loves dearly and who dearly loves and is concerned about his mother.

Upon receiving this note Dezrin's son took it to the Ottawa Police and the Nepean, Rideau, and Osgoode Community Resource Centre. Much to his surprise, they refused to investigate. This poor woman is essentially a prisoner of her health and the wilfulness of her husband who refuses to allow her to leave the home or to receive visitors despite her clear wishes to the contrary. Dezrin's son had hoped, a visit by one of the agencies, or an investigation would cure this situation. When this did not happen, he tried to arrange a visit and obtain legal counsel through the Nepean, Rideau and Osgoode Community Resource Center.

While recording his conversation with the Centre he found that legal counsel would not be forthcoming. The representative repeatedly and denied this help. She admits that this is the Centre's decision. However, in a later affidavit, a representative denies that the Nepean, Rideau and Osgoode Community Resource Centre ever declined to provide counsel. Something is wrong when an agency set up to help someone in this very type of situation is making contradictory statements while refusing to supply needed services that fall under its jurisdiction.

Clearly, Dezrin needs help. Society cannot allow our elderly and disabled to be virtually held prisoner, with no outside persons allowed to simply do a wellness check or to just visit and say hello. This is especially true when the disabled person has written a request for assistance.

———

Nepean, Rideau & Osgoode Community Resource Centre Ignores Elderly Woman's Rights

An ill-treated elderly woman's cry for help goes ignored by a social service agency in Canada's capital. Neglected by her husband, she was also barred from meeting her son, by this same husband. Although responsible social workers were informed, shockingly, no proper action was taken towards the matter.

Elderly woman abused and mistreated

The woman, Dezrin Carby-Samuels, living in Ottawa had been continuously neglected by her husband and had eventually become helpless and disabled. After learning about the incident through neighbours, the Nepean, Rideau & Osgoode Community Resource Centre was approached by the woman's son seeking help after the police "declared" no abuse had happened. Even though the woman had written a note addressing her son about the abuse she was facing, the social workers had overlooked the message for help in the note.

Clear evidence ignored

Horace, the man said to have abused her, and her husband also has a history of violence with clear evidence of an incident where he had attacked and wounded his son with a knife. This history of domestic violence was ignored by the social workers while also ignoring the transformation of a well-groomed elderly woman to being frail and disabled.

Ripped off of her human rights

As seen in the video, the social worker appointed in the situation, Ms. Timmons, confirms that for the meeting at the community center that was arranged the presence of a lawyer for Mrs. Dezrin was not allowed by the Community Resource Center. Even though this was the case Ms. Timmons would later sign an affidavit that she was not the person who refused to allow the presence of a lawyer but the decision was taken by Ms. Dezrin.

Ms. Dezrin has not been given proper medical care under her husband's auspices and her son remains concerned about the whole situation. Although the woman has requested to see her son once every week, the community center has ignored Dezrin's request to see her son. After the meeting that was arranged in the community center, this center had informed that it would not facilitate any more meetings between the son and the mother.

Is our future secure?

This shocking situation leaves all of us speechless and wondering what would happen to elderly women in society if even the police and the social workers do not work towards their betterment. A mother and a son being separated from each other and not letting the son meet his mother who is being ill-treated is cruel and heartless. This leaves all of us questioning the law and humanity prevailing in this society.

Chapter 5

Courts

Editorial comment

There are ethical and noble judges within Canada's court system. However, the Mandela Effect has subverted our court system into the substantive hands of an unseen "Deep State" as alluded to by U.S. President Donald Trump, and it is the "Canadian branch" of an apparent transnational Deep State which has sought to perpetuate social justices which include those directed against Dezrin Carby-Samuels. And this "Deep State" alluded to by Dr. Michael Salla has seized control of our Court system through Judges who operate on behalf of an apparent demonic-satanic agenda. Dr. Salla refers to this threat against human sovereignty as a manipulative-alien-political-industrial-military complex.

Through the apparent "Mandela Effect", an apparent Deep State executed a veritable Kangaroo Court which ignored all evidence presented by Raymond Carby-Samuels which presented a pattern of abuse against the civil rights of him and his Mother. The Courts then correspondingly accepted all verifiable lies presented by John Summers as the lawyer for the manipulative alien personae of "Horace" as the truth and then threw out the case. The Judges who sided with Raymond Carby-Samuels were subjected to isolation. To add insult to injury, the Archontic Judges presiding over the courts ruled Raymond to be a "Vexatious Litigant" for having sought to protect his Mom from a well-documented pattern of abuse in Raymond's testimony.

It is this kind of corruption which is seizing control of all levels of government in Canada and Justin Trudeau is not the instigator of it. Rather, he's simply an apparent public face of the same behind-the-scenes manipulators who condemned Ms. Dezrin Carby-Samuels, to a life of perpetuated abuse and Raymond to a life without his Mother.

———————

Canada's Supreme Court Judges Perpetrate Corruption, Iniquity When Not Under Spotlight

When the Judges of the Supreme Court are facing a decision that is being actively covered by Canada's mass media, you can just about always expect that they will be guided by the highest standards of fairness and equality which is the basis of the Canadian Charter of Rights and Freedoms. The notable decision of the Supreme Court under a strong media spotlight include decisions of gay marriage, and Métis rights.

However, having taught law, I can tell you that when not under the media spotlight, Canada's Supreme Court is nothing short of a cesspool of iniquity and corruption.

There is simply no callous act or pain and suffering that's too atrocious for these Judges to act out.

Since over 99% of decisions made by the Supreme Court enjoy no media coverage, over 99% of the time you can rest assured that the Supreme Court will act out its oppressive, colonial, elitist, bigoted and racist mentality to any decision which comes before it.

The Judges of the Supreme Court use the media spotlight to their full advantage. They make good decisions under the media spotlight so that the idea that they could be making evil and oppressive decisions on cases not under media attention will be farthest from the minds of most Canadians.

Canadians through the media see the "good side" of the Supreme Court while the demonic underbelly of the Supreme Court goes unnoticed.

One example of a case that poignantly shows just what kind of evil the apparent demon-worshipping Judges of Canada's Supreme Court of Canada are up to is a case against an Ottawa elderly black woman named Dezrin Carby-Samuels.

The demure 5' Dezrin began to suffer profound domestic violence at the hands of her strapping 6'4" husband starting in January 2013.

She wrote a note to Raymond, her son, that she was being abused.

The abusive father responded by hiring a dirty cop to cover-up matters of abuse and to prevent the son from further protecting his mother from abuse.

The result of this abuse is that Dezrin had lost the ability to walk, write and talk.

The son took the matter to court and won a default judgment on 11 February 2016 from Judge Patrick Smith.

But that's when things get even more "interesting". Marcella, the "sister" wanted her brother "out of the house" because she wanted to be the sole inheritor of family assets.

So, she endorsed the hiring of a dirty lawyer who graduated from the University of Ottawa Law School. This lawyer is affiliated to a University of Ottawa "secret society" of lawyers, judges, and members of the police who then perpetuated a process of ignoring not only Ontario Rules of Civil Procedure but a slew of other laws and ethical conduct reaching into the areas of the Canadian Charter of Rights and Freedoms.

Three of these apparent corrupt lower court judges include Sylvia Corthorn, Pierre Roger and Senior Justice McNamara.

Every time Raymond got a decision in his favour by a "regular" judge one of these apparent "secret society" judges would intervene to quash the decision through veritable Kangaroo Courts.

Judges of the Ontario Court of Appeal has proved to be in league with a fifth column of demonic judges in Ottawa's Superior Court that all sought to ignore the rules of law and equity, which, if applied would have spared Dezrin from further abuse and granted her desire to be reunited with her son that she had not been able to see since 15 June 2015.

So, by the time Raymond brought his Leave to Appeal to the Supreme Court, there was a record number of irregularities which should have easily led to the Supreme Court granting Raymond's sought Leave to Appeal.

But alas, since this case was not in the mass media spotlight, Supreme Court Judges had no interest in defending Dezrin from the abuse that Raymond sought to liberate her from.

Furthermore, since Raymond is black and was not a lawyer, the Supreme Court Judges were further offended that he did not pay the $100,000 plus a retainer that he "ought to have paid" if his Leave of Appeal went through a lawyer. Raymond's Leave to Appeal passed the "presentation test" in flying colors. Indeed, legal clerks at both the Court of Appeal for Ontario and the Supreme Court of Canada had remarked to Raymond that his filings were presented much better than many lawyers. However, it is apparent that no matter how well Raymond presented a system of corruption and irregularities executed through Lower 'Kangaroo Courts' without any media spotlight, Raymond had no chance of being able to liberate his mother from the heinous abuse and neglect by her husband.

It's time that we as Canadians begin to take an interest in the kind of atrocities that are taking place through our court systems in general and in particular behind closed doors of Canada's Supreme Court.

It's time that we as Canadians begin to furthermore take interest in a network of demons that is operating as judges and seeking to undermine basic human decency along with social justice, equality, freedoms, civil rights and the rule of law.

University of Ottawa Human Sacrifice Plot Against Disabled Woman Unmasked

I'm about to tell you something so unbelievable but true.

For over three years now, it appears that a group of judges at the Ontario Superior Court of Justice in Ottawa who are are all alumni of the University of Ottawa, Faculty of Law have been coordinating an apparent human sacrifice conspiracy against an Ottawa woman named Dezrin Carby-Samuels who has been severely disabled as a result of the activities of these judges.

In a nutshell, "human sacrifice" is a reputed activity of "non-human entities" who have coordinated and then reinforce the promotion of certain people into positions of power provided that they show their "loyalty" to the non-human entities when called-upon. The most vulnerable members of our society are targeted for "human sacrifice". The most heinous, barbaric acts of cruelty, torture, and destruction, are a part of a "human sacrifice" ritual.

The alleged practice has taken place since the earliest and most tyrannical societies came into existence on our planet Earth. In these societies, demonic aliens elites sought to worship demonic aliens as their God or gods that often brought technology that would then be used to support military oppression and torture.

Unfortunately, Dezrin Carby-Samuels, like so many vulnerable people on our planet is being targeted by non-human beings which can appear as "people". But these "people" are in no way human.

Dr. Michael Salla referred to such entities as 'shape-shifters'. David Icke has further described such entities to be reptilian that operate from a different dimension that reaches into ours.

Such victims like Dezrin include children who go missing as targets of alien abduction (or become victims of pedophile rings) to homeless people on the street who from time to time appear to be been chosen by the non-human handlers as targets of apparent human sacrifice rituals.

My name is Jesse, and I'm an investigative journalist. Since 2015 I have watched the bizarre activities at the Ottawa courthouse at 161 Elgin Street.

I have also investigated activities by non-human entities which include alien abductions. But I never expected that my investigation about Dezrin's plight would take me to apparent non-human interference at the Ottawa courthouse through judges working in tandem with Ottawa lawyers John E. Summers and Jeremy Wright of the City of Ottawa.

Jeremy Wright is an apparent ringleader of the University of Ottawa psychopaths, somehow recruited to perpetuate demonic torture against Dezrin.

Jeremy Wright in his official capacity works to defend Bordeleau's ragtag gang of dirty cops who sought to block Raymond from getting help for his Mom for more than three years.

In one instance, when a Small Claims Court judge was just about to enable Raymond to see his Mom, Mr. Wright gave some weird "wink" at a Judge sending him into an immediate panic leading him to immediately reverse his inclination to assist Raymond in helping his Mom. Mr. Wright is a highly secretive lawyer embedded into the City of Ottawa as an apparent handler for a University of Ottawa "rogue group".

It's notable that while one set of judges at the Ottawa courthouse would seek to liberate Dezrin Carby-Samuels, from profound abuse and torture that she has been experiencing at the hand of her husband, the "rogue group" would seek to perpetuate it.

The rogue group is made up of all members of the University of Ottawa alumni community. This group was reinforced by an apparent dirty cop named Detective Robert Griffin and a lawyer named John E Summers, who is the alleged lawyer for Dezrin's husband against Dezrin's son.

The funny thing is that Dezrin's husband can in no way afford Mr. Summers. When Raymond asked Mr. Summers, who he works for and pays his bills, he refused to say.

There is zero chance that Dezrin's retired husband who struggles to pay his bills could afford the legal services of John Summers who has been practicing law since 1999 and worked to perpetuate his abuse for more than three years at a pay rate of more than $300 per hour.

We, therefore, have 100% conclusive evidence that someone or more likely a "group" without any empathy for the plight of Dezrin in conditions of abuse is paying a University of Ottawa, trained lawyer who is getting the support of judges and others ALL directly affiliated with the University of Ottawa.

I don't believe in such coincidences.

But every time Dezrin was about to be liberated, another set of judges who simply ignore all the evidence and case law that Raymond presented.

Finally, one Judge named Sylvia Corthon, decided that she was going to "seize" the case, and declared not only Summary Judgement against Raymond, but also declared him to be a Vexatious Litigant.

It became apparent that Sylvia Corthorn had "seized the case" to prevent another judge who is not a member of an apparent University of Ottawa demon worshiping group from trying to again help Dezrin.

You see, Raymond, who is Dezrin's son has sought to liberate his Mother from abuse as any loving and responsible son would want to do.

One of my favourite shows is Murdoch Mysteries like so many other Canadians. One of my favourite parts of Murdoch Mysteries is when Detective Murdoch connects criminal suspects by tying a common association with each other using a blackboard in his constabulary office.

Thinking of the Detective Murdoch character I decided that I was going to try the same technique to figure out an apparent bizarre pattern taking place against Dezrin Carby-Samuels.

However, I didn't expect to find anything though this exercise. But to my amazement, I did.

All three Judges at the Ottawa courthouse that have worked with Ottawa lawyer John E Summers to perpetuate abuses against Dezrin are all University of Ottawa alumni.

These judges are Pierre Roger, Justice Sylvia Corthorn and Regional Senior Justice James MacNamara.

None of the three judges at the Ottawa courthouse who had sought to act fairly and support the liberation of Dezrin are connected with the University of Ottawa.

The judges who acted to spare Dezrin are Justice Patrick Smith, Justice Callum MacLoed and Justice Robert Beaudoin.

I have provided a screenshot proof of an apparent coordinated pattern of bizarre judicial decisions by the University of Ottawa alumni at the Ottawa courthouse.

There's a very distinct pattern of psychopath behaviours by three judges at the Ottawa courthouse with shared ties to the University of Ottawa that is extremely distinct from the behaviours of judges who aren't connected with the University of Ottawa. My screenshot shows the distinctive affiliations of legal "actors" in this matter.

Coincidence? I think not.

I then took my "theory" that there's "fifth" column of Judges who are seeking to subvert civil and human rights in resistance to the Canadian Charter of Rights and Freedoms to different Faculties of Law across Canada to get their reaction. Only the University of Ottawa, Faculty of Law members were hostile to the notion. It was almost as if they were hypersensitive based upon their complicit behaviour.

Could the University of Ottawa be home to the psychopaths who refuse to let go of their on-going abuse and torture against Dezrin Carby-Samuels?

Are we witnessing a human sacrifice ritual that has sought to seize and perpetuate Dezrin's abuse?

Is Dezrin, one of the possibly many people who have been subjugated to abuse in Ottawa, as a result of a "human sacrifice ritual"?

And guess where John E Summers attended law school? You would be right if you said the University of Ottawa.

I then became more intrigued. I then looked up Ottawa's Chief of Police Charles Bordeleau's background whose Office supported the dirty cop that forcibly separated Raymond from his Mother.

Once again we have a perfect match. Bordeleau also graduated from the University of Ottawa and received an award from the Telfer School of Management (screenshot attached).

After Bordeleau, dirty cop orchestrated Raymond's forcible separation from his Mother, who has suffered from profound domestic abuse, Dezrin lost the ability to walk, talk or write.

After months of unlawfully being prevented from seeing his Mother, Raymond filed an Emergency Motion at the Ottawa courthouse on December 2015.

Raymond appeared before the University of Ottawa, Faculty of Law graduate Justice Pierre Roger.

At first, Justice Roger was going to grant Raymond's requests, seeing as he began to say "no harm in it".

But that's when things began to get bizarre. Someone from the judge's chambers interrupted Judge Roger's deliberation.

When Justice Roger came out of this "meeting" he was a different person, declaring the matter "personal to him" and that he would say "no" to Raymond seeing his Mom and checking on her well-being.

Raymond persevered and eventually got a Default Judgement from Justice Patrick Smith, who has no affiliation with the University of Ottawa.

Justice Patrick Smith, who is a member of the Lakehead University community, granted Raymond's requests through an order dated 11 February 2016.

But shortly after, John E Summers, who was a top graduate of the University of Ottawa entered the picture. He began to manufacture and support countless obvious lies to justify continued forcible separation.

Raymond and his Mother last saw each other on 12 June 2016.

John E Summers' lies are easily transparent to any fair-minded judge. So, John E Summers needed "help" if he was going to perpetuate Dezrin's abuse.

John E Summers got that help when he and Raymond appeared in front of Regional Senior Justice James MacNamara, who threw out Justice Patrick Smith's Order to enable Raymond and his Mother to see each other, daily, so Raymond could ensure his Mother's care as she has wanted

Raymond tried to appeal that decision. But that appeal was then intercepted by an angry Justice Roger, who declared his interception to be a "coincidence".

I don't believe in such coincidences. It was quite improper for Roger to 'coincidentally' get the file. He should have recused himself. But, instead, Justice Roger "fined" Raymond $1500 for his Appeal.

When the matter was referred to Justice Callum Macloed, he was quite concerned about Dezrin's well being and directed John E Summers on 24 March 2017 to obtain independent verification to ensure Dezrin has not been held a prisoner against her wishes. On our "Murdoch blackboard," Justice Macloed is a graduate of Queens in Kingston, Ontario with no U of O affiliations.

John E Summers then sought to get the matter thrown out of Court. But his request was blocked by Justice Robert Beaudoin whose ties are with the University of Windsor Faculty of Law.

Then all of a sudden after this decision by Justice Beaudoin, the matter was then "seized" by Justice Sylvia Corthorn who like John E Summers, Justice Roger, Regional Justice McNamara and Ottawa Police Chief Charles Bordeleau are all University of Ottawa alumni.

Justice Sylvia Corthorn not only ignored all evidence and case law presented by Raymond but also ignored any support for Raymond articulated by the non-University of Ottawa Judges.

When Justice Beaudoin recognized her apparent judicial misconduct, by granting Raymond's request, that Justice Corthorn be recused from the trial, Justice Corthorn simply sped up her final rulings which were directed at preventing Raymond from his efforts to rescue his Mother from the "Hell on Earth" that she has lived for more than three years thanks to an apparent "University of Ottawa mafia" which has sought to perpetuate the abuse and torture of Dezrin Carby-Samuels.

Corrupt Ottawa Judges: Ontario Judicial Council Receives Complaint

*C*anadian judges, by and large, are champions of affirming the due process of law.

However, the letter below written to the Ontario Judicial Council suggests that there are judges who are less than ethical in their conduct.

In Ontario, two particular Justices have been responsible for breaching all sorts of judicial guidelines as a result of having been unduly influenced by the efforts of the Defendant who has sought to manipulate the judicial system.

As a result of the activities of these Justices, an elderly woman has been subjected to over one year of abuse and neglect by her husband who sought to keep her son away from championing the rights of his Mother. Evidence points to an apparent illicit relationship between these two Justices and the abusive husband, which have resulted in the Mother who has not seen her son in over one year no longer being able to walk, talk or write.

Ontario Superior COURT FILE NO: 15-66772

The Ontario Judicial Council - **OPEN LETTER**
P. O. Box 914,
Adelaide Street Postal Station,
31 Adelaide Street East,
Toronto, Ontario M5C 2K3
September 12, 2016

Criminal Misconduct - Justice P. E. Roger and The Hon. James McNamara

Dear Ontario Judicial Council,

It has been my experience that the great majority of judges in Ontario are steadfastly committed to the principles of balance, fairness, impartiality, ethics and the due process of law, even when judgments have not been in my favor. I have also observed Court administrative staff emulating the professional tone set by these judges.

However, bribery and collusion can affect the integrity of justice.

Justice P.E. Roger and The Hon. James McNamara, have been accepting "tribute" in exchange for favourable justice.

Does the Ontario Judicial Council support the practice of Judges meeting with a litigant in a case to then coordinate favourable justice for that litigant?

The Defendant was worried about possibly losing the Motion for Leave to Appeal to another Judge whom they could not unduly influence.

They then appealed to Justice P. E. Roger, who looked for, and seized control of the Plaintiff's Motion for Leave to Appeal in violation of

12.06 of the *Rules of Civil Procedure* and the following principles established by the Ontario Judicial Council.

3.1 Judges should maintain their conduct at a level that will ensure the public's trust and confidence.

3.2 Judges must avoid any conflict of interest, or the appearance of any conflict of interest, in the performance of their judicial duties

In the Eastern Division of the Superior Court of Justice, certain lawyers are also aware of The Hon. James McNamara's reported support for what is referred to as "donations".

"Donations" is also a word used by high-end escorts to avoid the legal jeopardy of clients paying for sex which is illegal. By making a "donation" prostitution laws can be circumvented. When a Judge correspondingly asks for a "donation" he or she seeks to circumvent the laws of s 119 of the Criminal Code of Canada against bribery and collusion.

Bribery of judicial officers, etc. - Criminal Code (R.S.C., 1985, c. C-46)

• 119 (1) Everyone is guilty of an indictable offense and liable to imprisonment for a term not exceeding fourteen years who:

o (a) being the holder of a judicial office, or being a member of Parliament or of the legislature of a province, directly or indirectly, corruptly accepts, obtains, agrees to accept or attempts to obtain, for themselves or another person, any money, valuable consideration, office, place or employment in respect of anything done or omitted or to be done or omitted by them in their official capacity, or

o (b) directly or indirectly, corruptly gives or offers to a person mentioned in paragraph (a), or to anyone for the benefit of that person, any money, valuable consideration, office, place or employment in respect of anything done or omitted or to be done or omitted by that person in their official capacity.

In Justice P. E. Roger's Endorsement dated 2016-09-07, he declared that he got the file for the Motion for Leave to Appeal as a "coincidence" – but it **was no coincidence**. Indeed, Justice Roger had specifically communicated to the Plaintiff in a very bellicose/hostile tone back in Fall 2015 that he regarded the matter as "personal". This admission violates his Oath of Office and Ontario Judicial Council guidelines.

His so-called "Endorsement" which levied $1500.00 against the Plaintiff seeking to see his own sick and disabled Mother is little more than a polemic that seeks to take vengeance against the Plaintiff for having received Justice Patrick Smith's Order that went against Justice P. E. Roger's commitment to his "handlers". In so doing, Justice Roger disregarded not only *s. 96* of the *Courts of Justice Act*, but Canadian laws which affirm the blocking of visitation access as constituting elder-abuse by the Defendant.

Justice P. E. Roger violated the integrity of the Superior Court of Justice for his self-aggrandizement and with the blessings of his accomplice The Hon. James McNamara. In the process, both these two Justices ignored all evidence and supporting documents by the Plaintiff in the execution of collusion and conspiracy.

Both these Justices have degraded the Superior Court of Justice to a corrupted modus operandi often found in the "Third World".

That is to say, a "Kangaroo Court".

It's apparent that Justice P. E. Roger and The Hon. James McNamara, have betrayed the high standards set forth by other justices of the Superior Court of Justice; and are acting as "operatives" of the Defendant. Justice P. E. Roger and The Hon. James McNamara, have committed prima facie criminal acts that require immediate investigation.

Justice P. E. Roger and The Hon. James McNamara subverted the honourable decision rendered by Justice Patrick Smith on 11 February 2016 that enabled and empowered the Plaintiff to see his Mom daily, as a result of Justice P. E. Roger and The Hon. James McNamara, having an illicit relationship with the manipulative Defendant.

Lacking a substantive Defence against the Plaintiff not being able to see his Mom who has been subjugated to abuse and neglect by the Defendant, criminal conspiracy became the only strategy to maintain the unlawful blocking of visitation access against the Plaintiff seeing his sick and physically disabled Mom who has sought to see her son.

Thanks for your consideration.

Regards,

HRC-S II

Corrupt Ottawa Judge Charges Son $1500 for Seeking to Care for Mom

When a judge charges $1500.00 against a son for seeking to care for his own sick and elderly Mom, you might wonder if our world is going upside down. But this is exactly what Justice P. E. Roger did. The son had complained to his father for having abused and neglected his Mother was then evicted from his parent's home against his Mother's wishes. The father has blocked the son from seeing his Mother since 12 June 2015. The son was then forced to sue his father for his blocking of access when he found out that his mother has lost the ability to walk, talk and write under his continued abuse and neglect, forcibly away from the protection of her son.

Justice P. E. Roger tried to arbitrarily throw out his Motions to see his Mom in fall 2015. However, the Plaintiff was able to get an Endorsement from Justice Patrick Smith to see his Mother on 11 February 2016. The father then hired a lawyer who contacted Justice P. E. Roger to quash Justice Patrick Smith's Order. This was a violation of 12.06 of the *Ontario Rules of Civil Procedure*.

Justice P. E. Roger lacks the empathy that's associated with who we are as humans.

The letter below further details apparent judicial collusion and conspiracy to subvert not only the *Rules of Civil Procedure* but also the *Criminal Code of Canada*, the *Ontario Courts of Justice* Act and the guidelines of the Ontario Judicial Council. To make matters worse, the nefarious subversion of judicial ethics also had an apparent accomplice -- the regional justice of the Eastern Division of the Superior Court of Justice.

Ontario Superior COURT FILE NO: 15-66772
The Ontario Judicial Council **OPEN LETTER**
P. O. Box 914,
Adelaide Street Postal Station,
31 Adelaide Street East,
Toronto, Ontario M5C 2K3
September 13, 2016

Criminal Misconduct - Justice P. E. Roger and The Hon. James McNamara

Dear Ontario Judicial Council,

Further to my faxed letter dated 12 September 2016, I respectfully request that the Ontario Judicial Council obtain copies of the entire FILE NO: 15-66772 - including a court transcript that the Plaintiff provided, to aid in your investigation.

An independent review of files submitted by the Plaintiff and the Defendant will corroborate the mishandling of this case as a result of the illicit relationship of Justice P. E. Roger and The Hon. James McNamara in relationship to the Defendant.

A 100% of the Plaintiff's evidence and Book of Authorities was ignored by Justice P.E. Roger and The Hon. James McNamara, as if the Plaintiff was "invisible", corroborating judicial prejudice. In contrast, the Defendant with the collusion of Justice P.E. Roger and The Hon. James McNamara was able to get Endorsements with a skeletal presentation without any independently verifiable evidence.

Furthermore, both Justice P. E. Roger and The Hon. James McNamara among other things accepted the truthfulness of Affidavits by the Defendant which declared that the Plaintiff "suffers from mental illness" – a complete fabrication.

Other evidence such as handwritten notes from the Plaintiff's Mom, Dezrin Carby-Samuels which stipulated "Dad Abuses Me" was also ignored in the haste of Justice P. E. Roger and The Hon. James McNamara to exonerate the Defendant.

In so doing, Justice P. E. Roger and The Hon. James McNamara subjected the Plaintiff not only to civil rights abuses, but also the Plaintiff's Mom to blocked visitation access which constitute elder abuse across Canadian jurisdictions and forcible confinement in breach of the *Criminal Code of Canada* for more than one year at the hands of the Defendant, Horace Carby-Samuels as a result of judicial prejudice and collusion.

The Defendant was not required to prove or substantiate anything, including allegations of "harassment" and "mental illness". The Plaintiff's evidence that the Defendant has used such allegations in Federal Court, which were thrown out by the presiding Judge was, once again, ignored, as ALL other evidence presented by the Plaintiff.

Justice P. E. Roger and The Hon. James McNamara over-turned the Order rendered by The Hon. Justice Patrick Smith on 11 February 2016 through collusion and criminal conspiracy. When Justice Patrick Smith was supposed to preside over the Plaintiff's Motion of Contempt, it is apparent after having correspondence with his secretary that he was taken off the subsequent Motion of Contempt as a result of orchestration.

Justice P. E. Roger's most recent Endorsement presented in my letter dated 12 September 2016 which subverted the Rules of Civil Procedure, the Ontario Courts of Justice Act and the principles of the Judicial Council further exposes the misconduct of Justice P. E. Roger and The Hon. James McNamara in the Eastern Division of the Ontario Superior Court of Justice.

Thanks for your consideration.

Regards,

HRC-S II

Ontario Superior COURT FILE NO: 15-66772
The Ontario Judicial Council - **OPEN LETTER**
P. O. Box 914,
Adelaide Street Postal Station,
31 Adelaide Street East,
Toronto, Ontario M5C 2K3
September 12, 2016

Criminal Misconduct - Justice P. E. Roger and The Hon. James McNamara

Dear Ontario Judicial Council,

It has been my experience that the great majority of judges in Ontario are steadfastly committed to the principles of balance, fairness, impartiality, ethics and the due process of law, even when judgments have not been in my favor. I have also observed Court administrative staff emulating the professional tone set by these judges.

However, bribery and collusion can affect the integrity of justice.

Justice P.E. Roger and The Hon. James McNamara had been accepting "tribute" in exchange for favourable justice.

Does the Ontario Judicial Council support the practice of Judges meeting with a litigant in a case to then coordinate favourable justice for that litigant?

The Defendant was worried about possibly losing the Motion for Leave to Appeal to another Judge whom they could not unduly influence.

They then appealed to Justice P. E. Roger, who looked for, and seized control of the Plaintiff's Motion for Leave to Appeal in violation of 12.06 of the *Rules of Civil Procedure* and the following principles established by the Ontario Judicial Council

3.1 Judges should maintain their conduct at a level that will ensure the public's trust and confidence.

3.2 Judges must avoid any conflict of interest, or the appearance of any conflict of interest, in the performance of their judicial duties

In the Eastern Division of the Superior Court of Justice, certain lawyers are also aware of The Hon. James McNamara's reported support for what is referred to as "donations".

"Donations" is also a word used by high-end escorts to avoid the legal jeopardy of clients paying for sex which is illegal. By making a "donation" prostitution laws can be circumvented. When a Judge correspondingly asks for a "donation" he or she seeks to circumvent the laws of s 119 of the Criminal Code of Canada against bribery and collusion.

Bribery of judicial officers, etc. - Criminal Code (R.S.C., 1985, c. C-46)

• 119 (1) Everyone is guilty of an indictable offense and liable to imprisonment for a term not exceeding fourteen years who

o (a) being the holder of a judicial office, or being a member of Parliament or of the legislature of a province, directly or indirectly, corruptly accepts, obtains, agrees to accept or attempts to obtain, for themselves or another person, any money, valuable consideration, office, place of employment in respect of anything done or omitted or to be done or omitted by them in their official capacity, or

o (b) directly or indirectly, corruptly gives or offers to a person mentioned in paragraph (a), or to anyone for the benefit of that person, any money, valuable consideration, office, place or employment in respect of anything done or omitted or to be done or omitted by that person in their official capacity.

In Justice P. E. Roger's Endorsement dated 2016-09-07, he declared that he got the file for the Motion for Leave to Appeal as a "coincidence" – but it **was no coincidence**. Indeed, Justice Roger had specifically communicated to the Plaintiff in a very bellicose/hostile tone back in Fall

2015 that he regarded the matter as "personal". This admission violates his Oath of Office and Ontario Judicial Council guidelines.

His so-called "Endorsement" which levied $1500.00 against the Plaintiff seeking to see his own sick and disabled Mother is little more than a polemic that seeks to take vengeance against the Plaintiff for having received Justice Patrick Smith's Order that went against Justice P. E. Roger's commitment to his "handlers". In so doing, Justice Roger disregarded not only *s. 96 of the Courts of Justice Act*, but Canadian laws which affirm the blocking of visitation access as constituting elder-abuse by the Defendant.

Justice P. E. Roger violated the integrity of the Superior Court of Justice for his self-aggrandizement and with the blessings of his accomplice The Hon. James McNamara. In the process, both these two Justices ignored all evidence and supporting documents by the Plaintiff in the execution of collusion and conspiracy.

Both these Justices have degraded the Superior Court of Justice to a corrupted *modus operandi* often found in the "Third World". That is to say, a "Kangaroo Court".

It's apparent that Justice P. E. Roger and The Hon. James McNamara has betrayed the high standards set forth by other justices of the Superior Court of Justice, and are acting as "operatives" of the Defendant. Justice P. E. Roger and The Hon. James McNamara has committed *prima facie* criminal acts that require immediate investigation.

Justice P. E. Roger and The Hon. James McNamara subverted the honorable decision rendered by Justice Patrick Smith on 11 February 2016 that enabled and empowered the Plaintiff to see his Mom daily, as a result of Justice P. E. Roger and The Hon. James McNamara, having an illicit relationship with the manipulative Defendant.

Lacking a substantive Defence against the Plaintiff not being able to see his Mom who has been subjugated to abuse and neglect by the Defendant, criminal conspiracy became the only strategy to maintain the unlawful blocking of visitation access against the Plaintiff seeing his sick and physically disabled Mom who has sought to see her son.

Thanks for your consideration.

Regards,

HRC-S II

Activist Applies to Supreme Court To Oppose Evil Ottawa Lawyer John Summers

John Summers calls himself a "Family Lawyer". But at least in one case, Mr. Summers can be described as a Family Destroyer.

The lawyer had told so many lies in Court designed to perpetuate the misery of Dezrin Carby-Samuels that it's a wonder how this man can sleep at night?

After more than three years of dealing with Mr. Summers lies and the Kangaroo Court he orchestrated with his conspirators on the Judicial Bench who all graduated from Summers' alma mater which is the University of Ottawa, Faculty of Law, Raymond has now skilfully navigated his legal plight to the Supreme Court of Canada.

Raymond has applied to the Supreme Court of Canada to seek a 'Leave to Appeal' in what would promise to be a landmark case against the control of our legal system in the hands of lying lawyers like John Summers, who seek to manipulate the courts with at times the willing support of certain judges who lack integrity.

John E. Summers appears to have sought to perpetuate the abuse of Dezrin Carby-Samuels by her husband and a dirty Ottawa Police Detective named Robert Griffin Jr. and Mr. Summers had done so with the apparent collaboration of the University of Ottawa fellow graduates Justice Pierre Roger, Regional Senior Justice James McNamara and Justice Sylvia Corthorn.

Isn't it time to put the efforts of cliques within our legal system that have sought to manipulate at the expense of the rule of law and human lives?

———✄⊰≋≋⊱———

Ontario Judge, Sylvia Corthorn: A proof that women can treat themselves crueller than men

Women might be their worst enemies after all—as in the case of physically disabled victim Dezrin, who has been treated with so much neglect even by her fellow gender.

Ottawa Judge, Justice Sylvia Corthorn in a recent ruling on an Urgent Motion request, utterly dismissed the civil rights of the disabled woman and her son Raymond, who is seeking to visit his mother to ensure her welfare and safety. This is after Justice Callum Macloed, on 24 March 2017, gave an injunction due to his apparent concerns for the safety of the elderly woman. He implored that a religious envoy—consisting of a rabbi, go along with the Defence Counsel's lawyer, Mr. John Summers, for independent verification to ensure that the woman "has not been held, prisoner".

While Justice Macloed—a male, showed that much empathy for Dezrin, Justice Corthorn, on the other hand completely disregarded this sanction. Quite surprisingly, her final ruling was in favor of the abusive husband who had subjected her to inhumane conditions and secluded her from her son. Raymond had attempted to rescue his mother from the hands of her captive, but met a brick wall, as Justice Corthorn blocked his attempt.

It is quite disturbing that despite the fact that Dezrin's husband had abused her to the point in which she is unable to talk, write, or even walk anymore—with all access to acquiring proper medical treatment and a proper meal equally inhibited, yet Justice Corthorn during her ruling determined that the situation was apparently not sufficient to be termed an "urgent matter".

One would think that the elevation of women into positions of high authority—where they are shouldered with the responsibility of making major decisions, would greatly promote the better treatment of women who are victims of insensitivity and immense discrimination. Yet the specific case of Justice Sylvia Corthorn has proven that it's never a matter of gender, as a female judge can be just as (or even more) oppressive as their male counterpart.

This case has shown that women, who find themselves in high rise political, judicial, and corporate positions, may become the female agents of oppression—just as Judge Corthon, has shown. It's safe to say that the discriminations women face in the Justice system here, and everywhere else in the world—due to callous and tyrannical minds, should never be limited to the male gender alone.

Justice Sylvia's action just goes to show that maybe, just maybe, women can sometimes be their own enemies.

———⊰❈❈❈⊱———

Ottawa Judge: Sylvia Corthorn Faces Criminal Charges

Sylvia Corthorn, an Ottawa-based Superior Court Justice who was appointed to be a judge on June 23, 2015, now faces criminal obstruction of justice charges. She is scheduled to be arraigned sometime early January 2018 in the Ottawa Courthouse at 161 Elgin Street.

The crime of obstruction of justice is considered a crime against justice itself since it undermines the validity of the legal system. Justice Sylvia Corthorn, has been linked to an on-going apparent corruption in the Civil Division of the Superior Court of Justice.

There have been reports about the corrupt activities of Sylvia Corthorn orchestrated Kangaroo Court against R. Samuels. Concerning this, R. Samuels had filed a Statement of Claims at the Ottawa Courthouse. One was against his father for having lied to the Ottawa Police that he "suffers from mental illness" to deflect Police from investigating his father's role is perpetuating abuse against his Mom which has resulted in her not being able to walk, talk and write. Another Claim was against the Ottawa Police for their illegal activities which include harassment against R. Samuels.

Justice Beaudoin, one of the ethical Judges at the Ottawa Courthouse had approved R. Samuels bringing a Motion to the Court to get Sylvia Corthorn kicked-off from presiding, any further, over specious Defence Motions for Summary Judgment and Vexatious Litigation filed by Bell Baker John E. Summers, Defence Counsel of the abusive father.

Justice Sylvia Corthorn on receiving the news that R. Samuels had filed a Recusal Motion which J. Beaudoin had approved became fearful that her plot to conspire with John Summers and the Ottawa Police in a separate court proceeding would be threatened by the Recusal Motion. She then decided to simply ignore due process of law that R. Samuels had been entitled to, and quickly rule in favour of John Summers and the Ottawa Police by endorsing Summary Judgment and declaring R. Samuels a "Vexation Litigant" so that she could also throw out R. Samuels' harassment claims against dirty cops at the Ottawa Police Service, that include Detective Robert Griffin and his co-conspirators who are responsible for also denying the rights of R. Samuels' mother who remains subject to spousal abuse.

Justice Corthorn went as far as to accept an apparent forgery of an affidavit filed by her friend John Summers that this Judge sought to evade from Court scrutiny. She now faces criminal charges for her role in a macabre plot which has resulted in R. Samuels' mother having been held hostage and abused for more than two years; and her conspiracy to use Vexatious Litigation as a means to assist her friend John Summers, and her friends at the Ottawa Police.

Obstruction of justice is a broad concept that extends to any effort to prevent the execution of lawful process or the administration of justice in either a criminal or civil matter. Obstructive conduct may include the destruction of evidence, the intimidation of potential witnesses or retaliation against actual witnesses, the preparation of false testimony or other evidence, or the interference with jurors or other court personnel. The purpose of criminal obstruction statutes – which every jurisdiction has, in one form or another – is thus to help protect the integrity of legal proceedings and, at the same time, protect those individuals who participate in such proceedings.

CHAPTER 6

John Summers

Editorial comment

The involvement of John Summers in this apparent Mandela Effect orchestration is highly mysterious. Here we have a lawyer working on behalf of his alleged client Horace Carby-Samuels, whose $300/hour rate Horace wouldn't have been even able to afford even when he was working a full-time job. But somehow was able to afford since March 2016? When Raymond asked Mr. Summers, who his 'real client' was who is paying his retainer, he refused to say. When Raymond then asked to meet with him to find out what was going on, Mr. Summers first agreed as long as he could take along three members of his law firm to such a meeting but then he rescinded his offer.

It was further revealed off-the-record by some lawyers in Ottawa that the Bell Baker law firm operates with "backroom connections".

It is apparent, therefore, that Mr. Summers' ability to spread a tissue of lies unchallenged by judges with University of Ottawa affiliations in the lower court is the result of Bell Baker's apparent illicit and clandestine associations with Archons.

Did Lawyer John Summers, a Police Detective and Judges Conspire in Mandela Effect?

My fellow human beings, let's talk about this so-called "Mandela Effect".

The Mandela Effect has not only been linked to all kinds of divergent experiences of pop culture like logos, but nowadays to changes in geography, histories like the JFK assassination and even to, changes in family members.

But, what if you were able to notice that one of your family members seemed to be in the process of being "replaced" by a" different person" as it began to happen in some kind of transition to a "new alternative reality"? In this "new alternative reality," the Statute of Liberty is on "Liberty Island" instead of Ellis Island, where it ought to be situated for having had a historical role the welcoming of new immigrants to the shores of America. In this "reality" instead of simply 'Starbucks' there is "Starbucks Coffee" among many other well-documented discrepancies.

Have you been wondering what the "Mandela Effect" is all about, and who might be able to provide some critical insights on it?

If so, you might wish to consider asking one particular Ottawa lawyer. This very bright and clever lawyer is John Summers and he represents Bell Baker LLP.

You see, when Horace Carby-Samuels and his wife Dezrin began to experience what we now appreciate as the "Mandela Effect", his son worked to countervail its efforts to change through various naturopathy treatments -- And it was working.

This somehow caught the attention of "a Group" who hired John Summers to pose as Horace's lawyer to fabricate court documents that Raymond "suffered from mental illness" to instigate the severing of contact with his parents.

Mr. Summers' paymasters wanted the experiments against the Ottawa couple to continue without Raymond's "interference" as part of Mandela Effect testing before expediting the Effect to the much wider population that we observe today regarding documented experiences of changes to family members.

Mr. Summers used his apparent connections with operatives to prevent Dezrin from seeing her son since 12 June 2015 to enable the "Mandela Effect" to continue. Dezrin essentially became a "Mandela Effect guinea pig".

This would have not occurred if Dezrin was able to talk, walk and write. However, it became apparent that the paymasters for John Summers did not see it in their interest Raymond's effort to protect the well-being of his parents.

After the paymasters of John Summers orchestrated an eviction against Dezrin's son, this poor woman lost her ability to talk, walk and write under apparent medical experiments associated with Mandela Effect intelligent design.

The Mandela Effect is the product of apparent intelligent design which began to be expedited in January 2013 with the help of the data from this couple associated with the work of the late Dr. Jerry Tenenbaum against Dezrin.

When Dezrin began to experience apparent symptoms of the Mandela Effect, she had been pushed to Dr. Tenenbaum, who for years collected data, but sought to provide no kind of treatment which would improve Dezrin's condition.

Dr. Tenenbaum's operatives got furious when Dezrin's condition began to substantively improve as a result of Raymond's intervention.

Since that time, Mr. Summers with the apparent support of a rich "Third Party" has sought to use lies to continue to prevent Raymond from rescuing his parents from an apparent effort to exploit an elderly Ottawa couple.

When Raymond asked Mr. Summers, who is paying his Retainer that he works for because his father in no way could afford to pay for years a more than $300/hour lawyer, Mr. Summers refused to disclose his paymaster.

Mr. Summers and his paymasters without any written endorsement by this Ottawa couple was even able to simply reply on an Affidavit supplied by Gorette Cleroux, his very own secretary, to pursue a new claim against Raymond as being a "Vexatious Litigant" simply because Raymond sought to verify the well-being of his Mother. Dezrin had suffered profound abuse, thanks to the efforts of Ottawa Police Detective Robert Griffin Jr., who conspired in Raymond's illegal eviction that was then enforced by the court presented lies of Mr. Summers.

Finding out who is paying Mr. Summers retainer bills as part of apparent extensive collusion may be key to appreciating the involvement of Archons, in prevailing "Mandela Effects".

It was the ancient Pagan Gnostics who sought to warn humanity about the Archons as the humanized face of a demonic alien artificial intelligence. The Pagan Gnostics simply referred to this threat as "artificial man" in texts that Christian elites under the influence of these demons would seek to cover-up.

It is, therefore, no apparent coincidence that when Horace sought to warn everyone during his apparent Mandela Effect experience that his apparent warnings were related to the "Fallen Angels" which the Pagan Gnostics link to "artificial man".

However, it is notable that the clever activities of Mr. John Summers to manipulate the Superior Court of Justice in Ottawa designed to perpetuate a Mandela Effect against an Ottawa couple who needed assistance from their son wouldn't have been successful if it was not reinforced by the corrupt activities of an apparent clandestine University of Ottawa alumni network which apparently includes Ottawa Judges and the Office of the Chief of Police.

Ottawa Police Chief Charles Bordeleau shares a past University of Ottawa affiliation to an apparent clique that has brutally victimized Dezrin to reinforce Mandela Effect related experiments against her.

Judges who were not graduates of the Faculty of Law at the University of Ottawa at the Superior Court of Ottawa all supported Raymond's efforts to get the support that Dezrin has sought from Raymond. In contrast, Justices McNamara, Corthorn and Roger, who are all University of Ottawa, Faculty of Law alumni, all sought to play their apparent roles in a "Mandela Effect" against Dezrin. Horace had begun to experience a rather violent alien presence seeking to "override" his human matrix with an alternative persona starting from January 2013. At the end of January 2013, the apparent alien presence of Horace took out a kitchen knife and held it against Raymond's stomach after Raymond expressed concern to Horace for having witnessed his mother being abused by him. As a result of trying to prevent himself from being stabbed, Raymond was sent to the Emergency Room as a result of his finger being nearly severed-off due to this violent act.

The alternative persona of Horace was violent and fixated on making humanity "members of a Bio-Electrical Union" as Horace began to rant about in his writings.

A spiritual medium in Ottawa alleged that Horace was taken over by a reptilian entity that sought to experience a human body.

This spiritual medium also alleged that Marcella Carby-Samuels (who conspired with John Summers in perpetuating Raymond's eviction against the explicit demands of Dezrin, to see her son) had also been taken over by the same entities.

Marcella also began to betray extremely violent tendencies in efforts to enforce apparent medical experiments against Dezrin.

Indeed, more and more families have reported loved ones being replaced by characters with a different recalling of family memories.

Horace, who had previously described his encounters with aliens through "out of body experiences" began to warn his son and anyone who he thought would listen about an imminent Extraterrestrial threat against Earth and humanity.

As Horace began to be taken over more and more, his true human identity could no longer make the same warnings against Archons.

It's becoming more and more apparent that Ottawa lawyer John Summers may be a key link to appreciating organized elite complicity in the "Mandela Effect".

There seem to be more and more representatives these days coming out about how an alleged "Mandela Effect" is creating rifts among family members. That is to say, it seems that family members from "the real Earth" are being foisted on identically appearing family members in this "new or simulated Earth", and who have a different recalling of past associations. The Mandela Effect traces its name from divergent experiences of when Nelson Mandela had died among people and ensuing discrepancies in experiences among people of material reality as suggesting evidence of human experiences of "alternative realities".

More and more people are noticing that some family members seem to be changing into different people right before their eyes, which naturally is causing alarm among those people who are referring to this phenomenon as a "Mandela Effect".

The role and relationship of Mr. Summers with well-financed paymasters suggest that the Mandela Effect supports an orchestrated elite agenda.

Horace's hysterical fears against aliens and the "Fallen Angels" in his spiritual struggles against the Mandela Effect suggest that it is part of an agenda that is alien and that is linked to a lower and cross-dimensional "artificial intelligence" referred to by the ancient Pagan Gnostics as the Archons.

Whether or not the damage caused by the Mandela Effect can be reversed to enable the reuniting of family members may very well depend on humanity discovering the role of John Summers and his paymasters against the activities of an Ottawa couple.

———————

John Summers: How this Ottawa Lawyer Covers-Up Crimes Against The Disabled

I call on The Honourable Jody Wilson-Raybould. Minister of Justice and Attorney General of Canada to investigate a sordid attack on not only the rights of a woman rendered sick and disabled by the unethical conduct of one lawyer, but the coordinated nature of this attack orchestrated by members of the University of Ottawa community.

Could a mafia-style organization operating from deep within the Faculty of Law at the University of Ottawa be seeking to profit from the manipulation of court cases at the Ottawa courthouse?

Could John Summers provide insight into what could be the greatest conspiracy in the modern history of court systems not only in Canada but of western democracy in general?

Could there ever be a more sick and twisted plot against any known conventions of human decency as the path presented by one Ottawa lawyer?

For many Canadians, hearing about a lawyer being unethical comes to no big surprise.

Indeed, in a CBC Doc Zone documentary, a few years ago, lawyers were "outed" as having an unusual concentration of psychopaths.

But, then there's John Summers who represents the downtown Ottawa law firm of Bell Baker LLP, that is situated right in front of the Ottawa courthouse.

Now, I have seen some treacherous and greedy lawyers in Ontario as someone who has been a member of the legal community.

But, here in Ontario, Mr. Summers could be in a category of his own concerning the apparent evils harboured within the legal community.

Have you wondered in all the experiences you have had with lawyers, just how low can a lawyer stoop on their single-minded focus for money with a lack of respect for human life?

I might have the answer for you now. You see, Mr. Summers and his paymaster had a problem.

Horace, his client was abusing his wife whose name is Dezrin Carby-Samuels; and Raymond, as any responsible son, wanted to protect his Mom from that abuse.

Raymond had sought to ask his Mom whether she wanted to temporarily move to a spare room in his south Kanata place to help expedite her medical recovery, which was not being helped by Horace's worsening pattern of irrational anger and violence at the home Dezrin shares with Horace in Kanata.

However, Mr. Summers didn't want Raymond interfering with the "right" of a man to abuse his woman who he owns as "chattel".

Mr. Summers' simple and effective "solution" to support Horace's apparent right to abuse and torture his woman as he sees fit was to manufacture a litany of lies designed to prevent Dezrin getting the support she desired from her son who had been her primary caregiver in support of her recovery.

Mr. Summers' apparent elaborate and grotesque lies published in his court submissions all sought to maintain and worsen a Hell on Earth for Dezrin.

John Summers' first of many lies that he submitted to the court was that "Raymond suffered from mental illness".

This lie was designed to proselytize the idea to local police that Raymond constituted a "danger".

There was also the lie that "Raymond sought to hold Dezrin and Horace hostage".

This was a lie also denied by Ms. Dezrin in writing, when she could still write.

John Summers then spread the lie to Court that both Dezrin and Horace wanted Raymond evicted back in late April 2015.

John Summers then lied that Raymond was seeking to somehow "force" his Mother to see him.

Mr. Summers further asserted the "medical competence" of Dezrin after more than three years of abuse at her Kanata-Katimavik area home without one shred of medical evidence to support his assertion.

When Justice Callum Macloed asked for independent verification of Dezrin's well-being, Mr. Summers first agreed, but within days reneged on the Agreement with another lie.

Mr. Summers then wrote to Raymond that he would at least obtain some medical information about Dezrin's condition. But that was over a year ago! Yep, you guessed it. Summers lied again.

Mr. Summers in 2017 became even more "creative" by alleging that Raymond got "banned" for calling Ottawa Ambulance Services in an incident that Dezrin credited for saving her life.

Raymond had approached Ottawa Ambulance Services and said there was no such ban.

Mr. Summers even went further by apparently presiding over the forgery of Horace's signature according to two handwriting experts in 2017.

Both handwriting experts assert that there is a 100% certainty that Horace's signature was subject to forgery.

When Summers apparently couldn't get Horace to endorse his lies the determined Summers put pressure on Ms. Gorette Cleroux, his secretary to fraudulently prepare an affidavit of more lies against Raymond concocted by Summers to perpetuate Dezrin not getting the vital assistance she wanted from her son against beat-downs by Horace linked to the abuse Dezrin had described.

However, all the lies of Mr. Summers at the Ottawa courthouse would have gone nowhere if it was not for Mr. Summers calling upon judges at the Ottawa Courthouse who all graduated from the same law school as Mr. Summers - University of Ottawa Faculty of Law.

Is it a coincidence that four judges at the Ottawa courthouse who ignored all of Mr, Summers voluminous lies were all graduates of the same law school Mr. Summers attended and the Judges who had sought to support the affirmation of the rights of Dezrin and her son to see each other were from other law schools?

I don't believe in such "coincidences".

Back on 11 February 2016, Raymond had successfully obtained a court order from Justice Patrick Smith, who is affiliated with the Lakehead University community.

But since that time, the judges who have sought to roll back this ruling are all alumni from the very same Faculty of Law as Mr. Summers. This suggests a coordinated action through a common criminal association with one another.

Justice Callum Macloed is an alumnus of Queens University in Kingston, Ontario.

This Justice had sought to support a path of social justice for both Dezrin and her son, and Justice Beaudoin, who also similarly sought justice in this matter had graduated from the Faculty of Law at the University of Windsor.

The apparent low-life judges who coordinated the seizing of the case from a path of justice for Dezrin Carby-Samuels are Justice Pierre Roger, Senior Justice James McNamara, and Justice Sylvia Corthon who are alumni from the University of Ottawa Faculty of Law along with John E. Summers.

Justice Sylvia Corthorn along with these other judges pursued an apparent criminal conspiracy designed to both ignore evidence presented by Raymond in defence of his Mother and support for Raymond by the non-University of Ottawa judges.

When Justice Beaudoin approved of a Motion to take Justice Sylvia Corthorn off the case, Corthon S simply ignored Beaudoin's approval of Raymond's motion and expedited her Kangaroo Court ruling.

Ms. Dezrin was a retired Registered Nurse who sought to spread charity to whoever she met. But thanks to Mr. Summers, Dezrin can no longer walk, talk or write today under Mr, Summers' lies.

Horace lost no time after Mr. Summers' paymasters had Raymond illegally evicted in late April 2015. Without Raymond there to protect her, the abuse got worse.

Within weeks, Dezrin lost the ability to walk, write or talk

Horace's abuse was confirmed by Dezrin Carby-Samuels, his wife, in her very own handwriting - that is, when she could still write.

This abuse ranged from a beat down to depriving Dezrin of the speech therapy she needed for a medical condition, to profound psychological torture.

Horace is so violent that one day on January 29, 2013, when Raymond had expressed concern in the kitchen to his father's abuse, seeing his Mom cry after another round of abuse, Horace decided to grab a kitchen knife to stab Raymond. In the process, Raymond, who sought to grab his knife to prevent him from stabbing Raymond in the stomach had one of his fingers almost severed by the knife.

It's plainly apparent here that Mr. Summers has sought to orchestrate a false flag conspiracy against Dezrin and her son with the organized support of the University of Ottawa Faculty of Law "mafia", which have sought to preside over a Kangaroo Court at its worse, and I ask readers to send emails and letters to the Attorney General to demand an immediate investigation.

Dezrin has been physically weakened by Horace's abuse and John Summers' coordinated conspiracy in this matter.

Ottawa Lawyer Prepares False Affidavit Regarding Ottawa Ambulance Service Blacklist

Just when you thought the law profession could not get any lower in matters pertaining to professional ethics, you might wish to think again. On Ontario Superior Court File 15-66772, Defence Counsel John

Summers prepared a rather interesting affidavit that "ambulance services have placed a block" against Raymond, the plaintiff in this case. At *The Canadian*, we reviewed a note in response to Raymond`s inquiry to Ottawa Ambulance Services, which completely denied any existence of such a 'blacklist.' This is yet again, one other apparent mischievous allegation spread by Mr. Summers in affidavits he has prepared.

Apparently, according to Mr. Summers, Raymond was being a nuisance because he had called Ottawa paramedics a couple of years ago when he saw his Mother lying beside her bed not breathing. Raymond called his father, who became the

Defendant in this case, who was not the least bit worried.

Thankfully, Raymond had the good sense to call 9-1-1 and Ottawa Paramedics had given Raymond instructions on exactly how to revive his Mother. These instructions included putting her on her side. Raymond, followed these instructions, and soon after Raymond`s mother started breathing again, just before paramedics arrived.

Raymond`s Mom was very grateful to her son as she described in a written note as 'saving her life`. However, it appears John Summers and his client have been 'not so grateful' by electing to slander Raymond for having sought to save his Mother`s life in the face of a bizarre passive indifference by Raymond`s father.

However, this is not even the biggest lie that Mr. Summers has sought to spread.

You see, since 12 June 2015, Raymond has not been able to see his Mother.

Raymond`s Mother back in spring 2015, handed a note to her son that her husband had been abusing her. Specifically, the note read, "Dad, Abuses Me." Raymond`s mother had hoped that by putting her abuse in writing, Raymond could then carry it to the police to relieve her situation of abuse.

However, Raymond`s father had a plan in mind, and that was to spread the lie that Raymond 'suffers from mental illness' which he used to get the police to remove him from looking after his Mother anymore, and since that time John Summers has spread the lie that 'Raymond`s parents don't want to see him anymore.' On 24 March 2017, Justice Macloed asked for what he described as 'independent verification' of Raymond`s mother's wishes to ensure that she was 'not being held a prisoner`. However, this endorsement was blocked under the auspices of John Summers who has continued to spread the apparent fraudulent representation concerning the wishes of Raymond`s Mother.

A photo of this endorsement accompanies this article.

You might ask why doesn`t Raymond`s Mother just run away from the situation of abuse and meet with her son? Well, unfortunately, that's not possible, because Raymond's Mother can no longer walk, write or talk, as a result of being forcibly separated from Raymond, who had been her caregiver who had also sought to protect his Mom from the abuse and neglect. Within weeks of being forcibly separated from her son in late April 2015, Dezrin, who is Raymond's Mom lost the ability to talk, walk and write in early June 2015 according to the Nepean, Rideau and Osgoode Community Centre. And, thanks to John Summers, conditions of abuse have been perpetuated under a plethora of misrepresentation.

CBC-TV's Doc Zone had once named lawyers as having a relatively high concentration of psychopaths. A psychopath is an ego-driven entity committed to pursuing a singular objective in pursuit of an objective for "success" irrespective of empathy in general or, specifically, how many lives along the way are destroyed. Unfortunately, John Summers has sought to pursue his activities in the courtroom regardless of the civil rights of Dezrin – a now chronically ill and disabled Mom – whose living Hell has been perpetuated by the tactics of deception lacking in a moral or ethical conscious associated with human decency as described by Raymond who we interviewed. We were told that John Summers has reportedly sought to "refrain from any comment" regarding the "Hell on Earth" that a sick and disabled elderly woman is being subjugated.

Ottawa Lawyer Perpetuates Psychological Trauma Against Disabled Woman

There are moments when behaviours of certain individuals tend to undermine the basic principle of humanity. However, when such behaviour is displayed by someone who is supposed to know better, then, eyebrows should be raised.

Ms. Dezrin Carby-Samuels, and her son, Raymond have both had to deal with countless abuse of their basic human rights and just when everyone thought that justice will be served, John E. Summers stepped in with his callous disregard for the desires of Dezrin and her enforced isolation by his client.

John E. Summers, a Bell Baker lawyer has gone to the extent of preparing a fraudulent affidavit and using other deceptive methods to deny Dezrin and Raymond the chance to even see each other since 12 June 2015.

The evil being perpetuated by John Summers clearly shows that people who are supposed to know better with regards to the application of the laws of the land can even stoop so low as to use lies and fraud to commit crimes against humanity. If nothing at all, John Summers should have realized that Dezrin Carby-Samuels is an aged, elderly woman who deserves nothing less than respect and reverence from society.

There is one thing that John Summers' callous disregard for the rights of Dezrin further proves and that is the fact that there is a very big difference between being human and a human being. This goes to show that one can be a human being alright and still behave in a way that is alien to humans who embrace empathy for each other. For a lawyer to be able to fabricate lies against an elderly woman and her son is simply a slap right in the face of law enforcement and our humanity.

Even though on the 11th of February, 2016, Justice Patrick Smith's Superior Court of Ontario made a ruling that Raymond should be allowed to pay daily visits to his sick and bedridden mother. However, John Summers in collaboration with Dezrin's husband, Horace, and daughter, Marcella have used dubious ways and means to prevent Raymond from seeing his sick mother. They even went to the extent of fraudulently tagging Raymond as not being sound mentally.

When a lawyer, in his right senses, decides to deceive the court to frustrate an elderly woman like Dezrin Carby-Samuels, then it is about time that well-meaning humans team up to support a petition for the disbarment of John Summers from further practicing law in the Province of Ontario.

John Summers: Ottawa Lawyer Undermines Justice for Elderly Women

Thanks to the activities of John Summers from the law firm Bell Baker in Ottawa an elderly woman's hope of ever seeing her son before she dies is fading. Ms. Dezrin Carby-Samuels had sought to see her son since 12 June 2015.

Raymond Carby-Samuels, who had witnessed the infliction of abuse and neglect by his father, Horace Carby-Samuels, who got Raymond evicted from his parents' home so that he would not be able to further defend his elderly Mom from that abuse.

Justice Patrick Smith granted a court order giving mutual access to Raymond and his Mother seeing each other on 11 February 2016 (documented in the above video). The abuse against Dezrin Carby-Samuels that worsened with the forcible removal of Raymond worsened the abuse and resulted in Dezrin not being able to talk, walk and write.

John Summers through unethical activities which is the current subject of a complaint to the Law Society of Upper Canada has managed to frustrate Dezrin's access to seeing Raymond, her son. John Summers' unethical activities include preparing a fraudulent affidavit that falsely accused Raymond of suffering from "mental illness". Mr. Summers has sought to support other such accusations without one iota of independently verifiable evidence as Dezrin's health has deteriorated.

As John Summers' deceit, deception and lies mount, Dezrin's health has gotten worse.

We ask for members of the public to take a stand against Bell Baker's lawyer oppressing the civil rights of a defenceless elderly woman and her son seeing each other through free speech that will help liberate Ms. Dezrin Carby-Samuels, from the elder spousal abuse that is being perpetuated by Mr. John Summers.

The law profession is supposed to be honourable and not to be used as a tool to deprive a mother of ever seeing her son protect an abuser who has seized control of her money to perpetuate abuse against her with the help of a lawyer who seems willing to support the lies that undermines the course of justice.

Ms. Dezrin Carby-Samuels, had been made an apparent prisoner of her own home thanks to the assistance of John Summers and his dishonourable activities.

Ottawa Lawyer Ignores Rights of the Disabled

It is widely accepted that physically disabled Canadians are entitled to equal rights and the affirmation of the human rights. This has been enshrined in our *Canadian Charter of Rights and Freedoms*.

That is why Ontario Superior Court Justice Macloed in an Ottawa on 24 March 2017 direction on a Motion asked John Summers to go with a religious envoy to visit the physically disabled client of his abusive client to find out who she wants to see to break her isolation.

For more than 500 days, John Summers' client has blocked visitation access and made his wife essentially a prisoner in her own home.

After consulting with his client. John Summers replied that his client would not allow either him or the court endorsed envoy to see his wife. Rather than Mr. Summers demanding that his client respects the court's direction as a condition of his continued service and in the interest of respecting the rights of a physically disabled person, John Summers elected to perpetuate his client's *De facto* criminal interference.

Help support an email letter-writing asking that he respects the rights of physically disabled Canadians not to be made a prisoner in their own home at the hands of abusers.

Thanks to John Summers, Dezrin's life has been made into a Hell in her own home for more than 500 days. She can no longer walk, write and talk thanks to the abuse involving forced isolation. Watch the above video for more information.

John Summers has helped to embellish the lies of "his client" which have included the fraudulent misrepresentation that Dezrin's son "suffers from mental illness" to justify her husband's desire to block Dezrin and Raymond, her son's desire to see each other.

Has An Ottawa Lawyer Helped Sell Humans-Out to Demonic Aliens?

Today, I'm going to tell you very shocking news about a lawyer in Ottawa. His activities beg the rather alarming question on whether he's part of a group of 'Archons' identified in the above video excerpt by Alex Collier that is part of an effort to sell-out fellow humans to manipulative aliens for commercial profit.

John Lash revealed on Metahistory.org that the 'Archons' appear as "regular people" but are controlled by a collective demonic alien artificial intelligence mind matrix which has been responsible for orchestrating wars and countless human suffering on our planet Earth.

These entities are not from our universe, but originate from a lower dimension that has reportedly sought to use its artificial intelligence to divide, rule, conquer and exploit spiritual-biological beings like humans who possess souls that endows us with higher dimensional consciousness.

The truly shocking activities of John Summers reveals apparent "fifth columns" in strategic positions of local police and among Judges who appear to be part of a "new slave trade" involving humans seeking to sell-out humans to the nefarious activities of Archons.

The most vulnerable members of human society which include "missing children", the homeless and the elderly are reportedly being exploited by alleged alien interests, and it appears that John Summers has aided and abetted a hostile agenda.

When Ottawa man Horace Carby-Samuels began to complain to friends and family about an "Extraterrestrial threat" his son sought to come to both his father's and his mother's rescue. Horace began to complain of aliens seeking to take control of his body through his mind.

The result of these reported alien incursions was that a normally mild-mannered Horace began to suffer from increasing apparent episodes where an alien mind would seize control of him which resulted in that alien persona inflicting sadistic abuse against his wife.

Raymond reported seeing his father's eyes roll in his head every time this apparent psychotic alien presence took over. During one of these episodes, the apparent alien that seized control of Horace held a knife against Raymond's stomach, which sent him to the Emergency Room when Raymond had sought to protect his mother from the apparent abusive alien presence.

An informer revealed that Horace was taken over by a commanding officer of an alien military command structure that sought to experience human emotions through Horace.

According to Alex Collier, the souls of humans are being "bottled-up" while aliens are seizing control of the bodies of human hosts. Horace appears to be one of the latest victims and it appears that we, as humans, have John Summers to thank in his continued efforts to "protect" Horace and Dezrin as the property of the aliens that have sought to use these two humans.

John Summers entered the picture just when Raymond sought to get help for both his father and mother who were being subjected to a violation of their human sovereignty.

Mr. Summers claimed to be working for Horace Carby-Samuels to keep Raymond away from both his father and mother. But after Raymond told Mr. Summers that this was not credible because his now-retired father couldn't even afford a lawyer working at over $300/hour, when his father was working, Mr. Summers then revealed that he was "not at liberty" to say who he was being retained by.

Similarly that Africans used to sell fellow Africans as slaves for commercial profit, Alex Collier reveals that humans are selling out other humans to enable demonic aliens to subject humans to various sadistic experiments.

Both Horace and Dezrin Carby-Samuels appear to have been subjected to alien abduction and related experiments and it appears that at least one Ottawa lawyer's job is to ensure that these experiments continue without any further interference from humans like Raymond.

John Summers' key role in all this has been to make up a tissue of lies that would then be reinforced by fellow Archons working at Ottawa Superior Court. These include Justices MacNamara, Roger and Corthorn who together used their mutual ties to an apparent "University of Ottawa" clique to sabotage efforts by other judges to support Raymond's efforts.

When Raymond back in February 2016 obtained an Order from Justice Patrick Smith to protect his Mom from the sadistic alien personae that had seized control of his father's body, John Summers and his apparent Archon associates expedited a false flag operation against Raymond to ignore all evidence of abuse by Horace while also seeking to declare Raymond to be a "Vexatious Litigant" for seeking to reinstate Justice Patrick Smith's Order.

John Summers' published lies in court documents include fraudulent claims of Raymond "suffering from mental illness" and being "blacklisted by Ottawa Ambulance Services." These lies would then be treated as "fact" by his fellow Archons operating as Judges.

John Summers' activities are a wake-up call to all humans of how our planet is being destroyed as a result of those humans who seek to support an apparent alien agenda against other humans who seek commercial profit and power under the hegemony of demons.

Ottawa Lawyer Oppresses Disabled Woman Through False Affidavits

The heights of wickedness that can be shown by a human being towards another person can only be imagined. There have always been reported cases of people putting others through various degrees of torture. However, those people mostly had certain things in common and that includes not being well-informed, the incidence of some mental disorder, and many others. It is therefore very rare to come across an individual who is well-informed, educated and expected to be an example for others in the society stooping so low to spread false information in affidavits just to win a case against a man and her mother.

The woman, Dezrin, has had to endure a very torrid time at the hands of her husband. Ms. Dezrin thought that her only hope of getting out of the house alive and kicking was to let her son Raymond know of what was going on. She, therefore, wrote a note for her son that read "Dad Abuse Me" and gave it to her son. Raymond also took the matter up and decided to rather involve the law enforcement agencies and the justice department. However, things just went from bad to worse as his dream of seeing his mother happy and lively again was squashed by certain criminal elements within the police service.

John Summers, the lawyer hired by Dezrin`s husband, has made it a point that mother and son must lose the case either by hook or by crook. He started by making claims that Raymond "suffered from mental illness" and as such shouldn't be allowed to be visiting Dezrin. He peddled this falsehood until Raymond was barred from visiting his mother in June 2015. Raymond has since that time not been allowed to even see his mother even after obtaining permission from the law courts.

Currently, there has also been another development in the case that all help in proving how diabolic John Summers can be.

In an affidavit that Mr. Summers prepared, he claimed that Raymond had been blacklisted by the ambulance service for some time now. However, upon further investigation, it was found out to be completely untrue.

Raymond had called for an ambulance when he found his mother lying in a supine position and not breathing. According to the 9-1-1 call that he placed at that time, he even stayed on the line for some time as the paramedics gave him instructions on what to do to resuscitate his mother. By the time that the ambulance came, the mother had already gained consciousness and up to this day, she says she will forever be indebted to her son for what he did that day.

For a mother to appreciate something that her son did for her, it comes as a hit below the belt to realize that John Summers has decided to falsify what happened on that day to win a case against an elderly woman whose constant abuse at the hands of her husband has rendered her immobile. This is surely the height of wickedness that can be shown by a human being towards another human.

Ottawa Lawyer Perpetuates Abuse Against Sick Elderly Woman

Is it true that the world is coming to an end?

This is the million-dollar question that many people have been asking for a very long time now and conspiracy theorists will straight away answer in the affirmative. A look at the situation involving an elderly woman, Dezrin Carby-Samuels and her son, Raymond being subjected to all forms of abuse both at home and even in the presence of the justice system makes it a bit difficult to dispute the fact that the life in this world is actually about to come to an end.

For some time now, Dezrin has been at the receiving end of abuse involving enforced isolation by Horace Carby-Samuels and daughter, Marcella Carby-Samuels. The cruelty that father and daughter showed to Dezrin was even enough to send her to her early grave. However, her willing spirit has kept her alive even though she can no longer speak, write or walk. This notwithstanding, a lawyer by the name John Summers seems to be the last straw that breaks the camel's back if something is not done immediately to correct the harm being caused to Dezrin.

John Summers, a Bell Baker lawyer, created an affidavit containing the fraudulent assertion that Raymond suffers from "mental illness". This lie was made to ensure that Raymond never gets the chance to visit his sick and bedridden mother.

What will compel a lawyer under oath to blatantly embellish lies against an elderly, sick lady and her son's desire to see each other? There are so many things that come into play when the apparent wickedness of John Summers towards Dezrin is discussed, and all points to the fact that society is losing its direction with regards to the acceptable practices. Old age is a stage in a person's life that is revered all over the world by both the young and the elderly in society. So it comes as a shock when a lawyer decides to connive with a father and daughter to execute abuse involving psychological trauma against an elderly woman.

John Summers' lies further came to light when the court found out that Horace Carby-Samuels had not filed his defence in 2016. Summers simply claimed that his client was not very conversant with the practices and procedures of the law courts. This shouldn't have raised any eyebrows since not everyone knows what to do when it comes to dealing with the law courts. However, Horace is a man who had the effrontery to dismiss his lawyer to present his account in a court case in the year 1990. So how can someone claim that such a person is a novice when it comes to court procedures?

Whatever John Summers hopes to achieve by subjecting Dezrin to such psychological traumas can never be understood. This is a crime against society and the earlier it is curbed the better it will be for humanity.

———— ❖ ————

John E Summers: Ottawa Lawyer Attacks Motherhood and Civil Rights – Support His Disbarment

John Summers will be the first to tell you that he supports the integrity and the commitment to family. However, he has an interesting way of showing it. For about one year now, John Summers has fought to ensure that Dezrin, a mother and Raymond, her son who loves each other, as close-knit mothers and sons tend to, never see each other again.

However, a lack of reasons for preventing a law-abiding son and mother from seeing each other has not stopped John Summers.

Mr. Summers has championed an unlawful effort by Horace, his client, to prevent Dezrin, his wife and, Raymond, her son from seeing each other. To this end, Mr. Summers has shown great skill in the use of lies and deception. These include John Summers' submission to the

Ontario Superior Court in Ottawa that Raymond suffers from ' mental illness' that's a threat to his Mother. After all, why rely on evidence when you can make it up?

Back in Spring 2016, John Summers also lied about his client being ignorant of court procedure causing him to not file a defence. This is the same client who was so confident about his legal skills that back in the 1990's he fired his lawyer at the time, and represented himself in Federal Court.

Most recently, on 24 March 2017, John Summers admitted to Justice Macloed at the Ottawa Courthouse that he has never even met Dezrin. In response, Justice Macloed asked that he and an envoy from a very established local religious organization meet with Ms. Dezrin, to re-confirm her desire to see her son that she has historically maintained since forcible separation by her husband back in April 2015.

In Horace's apparent fear that such a meeting would lead to Dezrin and her son seeing each other again, John Summers reported back saying that his client doesn't want either him, his own lawyer nor this envoy seeing Dezrin.

If John Summers were a lawyer of integrity, he would insist to his client that he and the envoy endorsed by the Court would be allowed to meet with Dezrin to confirm her interest in seeing her son, a condition of his legal services. However, Mr. Summers instead decided that he would accept his client's apparent perpetuation of abuse, neglect and forcible isolation which has resulted in conditions of profound psychological trauma against Dezrin.

Although Dezrin has been physically disabled under a pattern of abuse and neglect by his client, John Summers also admitted to Justice MacLoed that Dezrin remains mentally cable. However, John Summers has sought to ignore Dezrin's mental capability by going along with his client's desire to pursue what could be described as the criminal denial of Dezrin's rights to have any desire that she has to see her son ignored.

Is it okay for someone to abuse a spouse or significant other to the point of physical incapacity and then for that person to ignore the independent will of that human being? Is it okay for a lawyer to turn a blind eye to the cries of that human being who has been essentially forcibly confined by his client? Don't physically disabled people have rights in Canada? Don't lawyers have a professional responsibility to the court for the testimony of their clients based on integrity, and especially so when human lives are at stake?

How does a lawyer who claims to support the values of integrity, a commitment to family, and the rule of law required of his profession, then participate in what could be described as a de facto criminal conspiracy to ignore the civil rights of a mentally capable person that is affirmed by the Canadian Charter of Rights and Freedoms.

Does Mr. Summers have any empathy for Dezrin's plight and sovereignty as a human being, and Raymond's efforts to defend his Mom's rights? Or is Mr. Summers primarily concerned about getting his next legal retainer fees from his client, even if those fees could be construed as a form of 'Blood Money'?

We, the undersigned united say that no person who is so willing to ignore the pleas and cries of a defenceless elderly woman who had documented her abuse in writing when she could still write is fit to be practicing law in Ontario, Canada or anywhere else.

John Summers doesn't have the integrity to ensure that the rights of a Mother are respected in his effort to champion a sick and elderly mother and her son to never to see each other again. In the process, John Summers has turned his back on both human suffering and basic professional ethics.

We, the undersigned, deplore the professional behaviour of John Summers as an attack against the loving relationship of mothers and sons / their children everywhere that cannot be ignored.

Lawyers should not be allowed to support the possible criminal actions of their clients that threaten quality-of-life or lives of fellow human beings based upon a pattern of verifiable lies and deception.

The defence of a client's interest shall not include participation in either an apparent criminal conspiracy or support for activities that threaten lives through the calculated use of clients, and tactics of macabre deception.

We, the undersigned say that John Summers has thrown the legal profession into disrepute by being willing to perpetuate the infliction of conditions of torture and psychological trauma by his client against another human being, against the better judgment of the Court that has sought to endorse the importance of establishing the independent will of an abused woman.

We, the undersigned support the Law Society of Upper Canada disbarment of Mr. John Summers from further practicing law as a result of having breached professional ethical standards that have endangered and/or oppressed human life concerning fundamental rights and freedoms.

Chapter 7

Fred Carby

Editorial comment

This "man" did nothing to protect his supposed "sister" or Nephew. However, this particular life form like the other characters in this plot appear to be acted as some kind of sophisticated AI programs that have been programmed

Fred Carby: How An Evil Middle-Class Jamaican Turned His Back on Tortured Sister

The Christmas Season is about bringing families together.

And, since it's just before Christmas, let me share with you a story that makes me ashamed to be Jamaican. It is a story of how Fred Carby, an affluent and now retired Jamaican dentist who resides in Richmond Hill, Ontario, teaches us about evil and true hypocrisy.

As a result of Mr. Carby's apparent evil ways and hypocrisy, Dezrin Carby-Samuels, his sister, had been left to suffer in silence, now get this, since 20 April 2015, when Dezrin's son was illegally evicted by her abusive husband. The eviction was made totally against the will of Dezrin and left her to suffer in a "House of Hell".

In just a matter of weeks, Dezrin lost the ability to walk, write and talk.

In the accompanying photo, we see what Dezrin looked like just after a few weeks of being abused by her over 6ft and nearly 200 lbs husband back in 2015.

Since 12 June 2015, Dezrin had been blocked from getting the care that she needs that had been provided by her son. Fred turned his back on his sister who wanted to see her son help her toward recovery, Now, Fred could take apparent delight in his sister's destruction and he had no interest in any assistance his nephew could provide to help his ailing sister.

Arguably, a responsible brother would have intervened against the abusive husband in a manner to ensure that Raymond, his nephew, would be empowered to continue to prevent Dezrin from being subjected to abuse. But it soon became apparent that Fred Carby in a most bizarre way saw the turn of events in which his sister was getting abused as finally him getting the "upper hand" with God.

According to so-called middle-class Jamaican values, if something bad happens to you, it's not for anyone to intervene because that would be somehow acting "**against God**".

Why you think there's so much poverty in Jamaica"? It's because of "middle class" Jamaican values, believing that people who are poor or even suffer wife abuse is simply "**God's will**" -- apparently for Fred Carby, even if that wife abuse is happening against your sister!

But religion is only the beginning of Fred Carby's apparent irresponsible behaviour which resulted in Dezrin losing the ability to walk, write and talk. And what is even more shocking about Mr. Carby's complicity is that his mother when she was alive, she had told him to make sure that in any case of a crisis that he would be there to help his sister. However, when Dezrin needed Fred the most, Fred's "Red Eye" tendencies came out more than ever.

You might wonder what a "Red Eye" person is?

In Jamaican-vernacular, that's a person who sees your success; becomes jealous of it; wants that success to become your own; and then seeks to take delight in any misfortune that the "successful person" might eventually run into.

For Fred Carby, his "Red Eye" tendencies began when he was very young. You see, his father had lived in Portland, Jamaica and wanted Fred, his only son, to stay by his side there to help work the fields. He had let Dezrin, with his other daughters, to live, what could be regarded as a more comfortable and urban lifestyle in Kingston, Jamaica.

Rather than wishing success for his sister, for Fred, having to live in Portland, Jamaica, became an apparent longstanding source of resentment, even though that wasn't Dezrin's choice. This enraged him. He began to regard Dezrin as the "spoiled little princess" even though Dezrin, very much loved her brother and looked forward to always see him.

When Fred moved to Canada in the late 1950s, his jealousy grew when he saw Dezrin and her new husband driving a "nice car". He kept bugging Dezrin's husband to sell it to him not because he wanted it for himself, but because he just couldn't stand seeing his sister and her husband in his vehicle. When Dezrin's husband did sell the car that he loved to drive so much to Fred, Dezrin's husband was shocked to find out that Fred immediately sold it after purchase.

As I said, he didn't want the car himself, he just wanted the car out of his sight because of "Red Eye" jealously.

Years after, Dezrin with her husband moved to the States. Upon their return, they got a nice house in Thornhill, followed by another nice home in the southern end of Richmond Hill, Ontario not far from the current Express Highway 407 Toll Road.

When Fred saw the home Dezrin lived in after one visit he became furious because he could not afford to buy such a home after being subjected to a financially demanding wife which led to divorce. For more than 10 years, Fred refused to visit his sister, even though both of them lived in Toronto. This made Dezrin very upset who loved her brother.

When Fred learned that Dezrin and her husband were going to sell their home, Dezrin who has been a sister who loved her brother despite his "Red Eye" tendencies, consented to sell their home to Fred for a substantively discounted price.

So, when Raymond shared news of his sister being abused by her husband it is shocking, but predictable that Fred Carby didn't do the things necessary to spare his sister from a "Living Hell". He just allowed the abuse to continue and turned his back against Raymond, his nephew who sought to protect Dezrin from spousal abuse.

Fred Carby is an evil man who replaced love for his sister, other brothers would have with profound jealousy masked in pathetic hypocrisy over the years.

Words cannot fully describe Mr. Carby's utter complicity of a supposedly "God-fearing" "Christian man" who turned his back against his sister and nephew.

This story provides critical insight into why Jamaica suffers from so much poverty and social injustices. If Jamaica embraced "middle-class values" which sought to support one another in a spirit of love and empathy, rather than the evil and "Red Eye" tendencies of Fred Carby which is so profound that it can be inflicted against one's sister, Jamaica would be a much more gentle place supportive of the quality-of-living of all Jamaicans.

Why Ottawa's Jamaicans Ignore Police Abuses Against Disabled Woman

I'm a Jamaican living in Ottawa, Canada, and I can barely put in words just how ashamed I am of my people in this city.

You want to know about what kind of person the typical Jamaican is, read what I have to say -- and know about the place I sought to escape from, in my journey to Canada.

Unfortunately, "my people" who have come to this country have sought to keep true to their ways on the island, and that's where my dear friend Dezrin's story begins.

Since April 2015, Dezrin Carby-Samuels has endured unspeakable abuse and assault by her husband and with the support of Ottawa Police Detective Robert Griffin Jr.

I wished that Dezrin was never born a Jamaican because the Jamaican community is the only community that I know that could ever turn their back on such a woman.

If Dezrin was born in some other Caribbean island, white, South Asian, Muslim or any other community I can think this would never have happened.

For starters, my fellow Jamaicans in Ottawa are among the saddest of all Jamaican communities across Canada.

The first thing which worked against Dezrin getting any help from all the supposed Jamaican friends and relatives she has not only in Ottawa, including her cousin in Kanata; her so-called "brother" in Richmond Hill and the rest of her extended family in the States is that Jamaicans think that whatever bad happens to you in life happens because "God" wanted it to happen. Therefore, who are they to interfere in *"God's plan"*?

That's why there's no welfare system in Jamaica or other kinds of social support there that we in Canada take for granted.

So, as you can see, Dezrin could never rely on her fellow Jamaicans.

The second thing that is going against Dezrin is that she's not only Jamaican. She is also a woman.

Many people think that Muslim men are chauvinistic because of women who wear hijabs in their culture and the "sharia" laws.

If you think that, let me tell you about the typical Jamaican man and their place in Jamaican society.

In Jamaican culture, the man is **"King of the House"** which means men can commit routine sexual abuse, assault, and torture without neighbours blinking an eye.

When I used to live in a very affluent part of Jamaica in Kingston, the man living in the house beside me would lock-up in his wife in the house so she couldn't leave and beat her up almost every day. Yes, he developed a locking system to do that.

You might wonder how I would know this?

The wife's cries and screams every day and her confessions to me when he "allowed" her to venture outside.

This went on for years until I left for Canada.

That's the power that a Jamaican man has over his woman and even when he's in Canada he expects the same.

And last but not least, the third thing that Dezrin has going against her is that much of her so-called "middle class" Jamaican friends are so busy being paid informants by certain members of the police and other "shadow organizations" that they dare not seek to oppose a dirty cop like Detective Robert Griffin who could seek to cut off their access to money as paid informants digging-up petty dirt against each other. How much Dezrin may be tortured by a dirty cop is of no interest to them.

Do you think that Italians, Lebanese and other such communities in Canada would sacrifice one of their own to the likes of a dirty cop? Of course, they wouldn't. Such communities have too much respect for one of their own - a characteristic which Jamaicans don't have. "My people" have been selling out each other since slavery.

Thanks to Dezrin's husband having connections to local police, he has been able to continue the same kind of assault against Dezrin.

Horace, who is Dezrin's husband, first got Detective Robert Griffin to prevent the son from visiting his Mom since April 2015 even though she desired it.

Within weeks of enduring assault and torture under the supportive eye of Ottawa Detective Robert Griffin, Dezrin lost the ability to walk, talk and write.

When Raymond, Dezrin's son, got social workers from the Nepean, Rideau, and, Osgoode Resource Centre to intervene to help Dezrin, Horace blocked them from checking on Dezrin.

And all this was with the support of who I now know is a very dirty cop - Ottawa Detective Robert Griffin.

This low life cop ignored the cries of Dezrin, for her son.

Raymond turned to all of Dezrin's friends and relatives in the Jamaican community and they refused to "get involved".

Fred Carby, who is a now retired and formerly prominent dentist who lives in Richmond Hill also refused to get involved. What a nice guy, huh?

Raymond told me that this was particularly shocking because his Mother told him that Fred made a promise to 'Granny' to promise her to always be there for Dezrin.

But like other Jamaicans, he too repeated that "It's Horace's house so what can he do?"

Raymond told Fred about the note his mother had written him back in April 2015 that *"Dad Abuses Me"*.

Like the typical Jamaican male, he reacted *"So, what?* Men will be men. It's a man's right to discipline his wife. It's, Horace's house and, *"I won't interfere."*

Horace like the typical Jamaican man is violent. Did you know what Horace did when his son had expressed concern for his abuse against Dezrin? Back on 29 January 2013, Horace sprung from the kitchen table where he was sitting and held a knife to his son's stomach. His son grabbed the knife to protect his vital organs and in the process, his little finger was almost severed. Horace refused to call the ambulance for what he had done and Dezrin was too much in shock.

Raymond had to dial his phone for 911 with one hand as the other hand kept bleeding and was taken into emergency reconstructive surgery.

Horace likes to threaten his son and even his wife sometimes with a machete he keeps in the house that's about one meter long.

Fred's own high regard for defending the place of the Jamaican man "in his own home" was apparently more important than preventing his sister from being subjected to unspeakable abuse which transformed Dezrin from an able-bodied woman to a woman who began to smell of feces and who was assaulted and abused to the point of becoming disabled from that maltreatment.

Ms. Dezrin Carby-Samuels had been wronged by the very community she has sought to serve having become a nurse after graduating from University College in Kingston, Jamaica.

Ms. Dezrin was one of the first black registered nurses to ever be hired by a Canadian hospital after leaving Jamaica in the 1950s.

Ms. Dezrin paved the way for the hiring of other Jamaican nurses in Canadian hospitals having worked at hospitals in Toronto, Guelph, and Vancouver.

I am ashamed of the Jamaican community has turned its back against Dezrin. I'm ashamed to be Jamaican.

Peter Tremblay

Many people know of Jamaicans as having a culture of great food and with celebrations like the Caribbean festival in Toronto.

But under this facade is a Jamaican culture which turns its back on the plight of their own, whether the growing masses of the poor in Jamaica or whether it's a kind-hearted person like Dezrin who continues to suffer under the malice of Horace that is being perpetuated by an apparent pathetic psychopath who has no business being a police officer.

I hope in writing this that broader Canadian society and civilized people of the world will call Ottawa's Police Chief Charles Bordeleau and demand the resignation of Ottawa Police Detective Robert Griffin for his apparent support to conditions of abuse for more than three years.

In the above video, you will hear Detective Robert Griffin seeks to leave a message for Raymond. Later, Raymond was assaulted by Detective Robert Griffin in broad daylight at his Kanata home. The plainclothed Detective Griffin demanded that Raymond must not tell anyone about Dezrin's abuse.

So, there you have it, folks!

This cop didn't want to stop Ms.Dezrin from being abused. He just wanted to make sure that Raymond, who reported the abuse wouldn't communicate that abuse to friends or family.

Thankfully, Raymond ignored this illegal assault and threatening behaviour of this police operative and has sought to defend his Mother from the abuse that he has witnessed.

I also hope that Canadians demand that their local TV and other newspapers start getting the journalists to help spread further awareness of Dezrin's plight.

Thanks to my fellow Jamaicans, Dezrin has become bedridden. *She can't run. She can't hide or escape.*

In the above photos, you will see what Dezrin looked like when she was still able-bodied back in April 2015, at what she looked like when she was rendered disabled by Horace's and Detective Robert Griffin's apparent **"House of Torture"** in Dezrin's own home in Kanata.

156

My fellow Canadians and other civilized people, let us rally for Dezrin and liberate this disabled woman from her "Hell on Earth" courtesy of Ottawa Detective Robert Griffin and my pathetic fellow Jamaicans which include her brother and her abusive spouse.

CHAPTER 8

Robert Griffin Jr.

Editorial comment

Ottawa Police Detective Robert Griffin is a primary operative working on behalf of the manipulative alien personae or Horace and Marcella in the context of an apparent "Mandela Effect".

Detective Robert Griffin: How Ottawa's Dirty Cop Helped Me Abuse My Wife

PLEASE NOTE: The following article doesn't reflect the views of *The Canadian* or its writers

*A*re you an average guy who likes to abuse his wife?

After all, I'm Jamaican. I can't help myself.

Let me tell you about a great experience I had with an Ottawa cop who helped me abuse my wife and kept my meddling son from stopping me.

His name is Detective Robert Griffin of the Ottawa Police.

Back in 2015, I thought that I was in trouble when social service workers wanted to check and see how my wife was doing.

The social service workers were going to testify against me with my son in Court about how I have been keeping basic medicine and other stuff they wanted to deliver to my wife.

That's when Detective Robert Griffin saved the day.

He marched down there like any guy who shares my views on the right of a man to do what he wants in his home and told those social service workers to back off.

Too bad that my wife can no longer walk, talk or write. Hey, it's not my fault she can't take any action.

She kept crying to see her son. Boohoo! Give me a break!! But thanks for the moral support of Detective Robert Griffin and his friends down at the Ottawa Police that will never happen.

Ottawa Cop Helps Man Abuse His Wife for Years

have you wondered why you haven't seen Dezrin Carby-Samuels since 2015?

The photos above show what Dezrin had looked like before Ottawa Police Detective Robert Griffin entered the picture and what Dezrin looked like thanks to the "wonderful" activities of this Detective.

Ms. Dezrin was well known for smiling and having a pleasant conversation for everyone who she came into contact with on her frequent shopping excursions all over Kanata where she has lived since the mid-1980s and also in many other parts of the city.

Thanks to Ottawa Police Detective Robert Griffin, Dezrin has been rendered completely disabled from a perpetuated context of abuse.

You see, back in April 2015, Raymond, who is Dezrin's son presented a note from his mother that read "Dad Abuses Me."

Ms. Dezrin gave the note to her son, hoping that she could get relief from the police.

Ottawa Police Detective Robert Griffin's reaction to the note was not to help protect Dezrin from her abusive husband. Rather, not only did he orchestrate the eviction of Dezrin's son against Dezrin's wishes, but also threatened social service agents led by Alison Timons to not only not testify in Court against Dezrin's husband as they had promised but not to further have contact with Raymond in his efforts to help his Mother.

When Raymond found out back in mid-June that his Mother had just lost the ability to walk, write and talk, Raymond did what any loving and responsible son would do. Raymond tried to reach his Mom to help her as he promised he would when he last saw his Mom on 12 June 2015. During that last Meeting at the Nepean, Osgoode and Rideau Community Centre, Dezrin communicated to Raymond as best as she could that she wanted her son's help.

But on 15 June 2015 Detective Robert Griffin stormed down to this social service agency and demanded that they help ensure that would never happen again.

This evil cop then went to Raymond's new residence in Kanata and told him that he was not to share information on Dezrin's abuse with anyone.

One of his threats, was in broad daylight in plain sight of witnesses who asked Raymond if he needed help against the plain-clothed Detective fashioning his 'stubble' look.

You might ask, what motivates a supposed law enforcement officer to work for the "dark side" of such an apparent evil as he has perpetuated against an innocent Mother as Dezrin who has served her country so well as a Registered Nurse and volunteer?

Is Detective Robert Griffin a psychopath with certain similarities to the character Hannibal Lecter? Or is Detective Robert Griffin just a low life that likes to prey on the elderly? Is there money involved, and if so, how much?

Is Detective Griffin just an operative of some kind of corporate-controlled experiment which they are "testing" on Dezrin? Indeed, some whistleblowers allege that certain prison population away from prying public eyes have been subjected to unethical medical experiments.

What we know here for sure is that Dezrin Carby-Samuels needs the help of her community in freeing herself from the criminal conspiracy that this so-called "Detective" has orchestrated.

Ms. Dezrin has been rendered completely disabled as a result of the spousal abuse she has documented and which this Detective has perpetuated.

Ms. Dezrin, therefore, cannot run, and she cannot hide. She lives in a Hell on Earth. She has wanted to badly see her son. But the evil Detective ignores her crises and despair.

But is the public, who reads this article, much better who will also undoubtedly not think twice about not helping Dezrin?

For more than three years now, Dezrin remains rendered prisoner by apparent demons and a system complicit in a heinous evil orchestrated by one of Ottawa's "finest".

Where are we coming to as a world when men and women in positions of authority can turn their backs on the reckless conduct of apparent demons in positions of authority?

Listen to the above video of this so-called Detective when he sought to call Raymond to "have a chat" about perpetuating the cover-up of Dezrin's abuse.

Where are we going to, as a society when these kinds of men (and women) are promoted to senior ranks of organizations that are supposedly there to protect "law and order".

The irony is that it is such evil men and women are behind the breakdown of our societies, including law and order, into the sick and twisted world which twisted minds seek to bring into reality and that we as humans must oppose its manifestations.

Let Dezrin be the first among many more of us humans that we can rescue from the demons who, lacking empathy, ethics or decency are destroying everything that we value.

Ottawa Police: Detective Robert Griffin Sued for Unlawful Activities

We like to believe that the police remain impartial and uphold the law, but as can be seen from the case to be brought against Detective Robert Griffin, this is not always true. The behavior of this officer could be compared to that of the 'dirty cops' we see in movie dramas.

The plaintiff laying the charge against Detective Griffin, Mr. Raymond Carby-Samuels, is currently appealing to members of the public to come forward in support of his case if they have experienced similar treatment on the part of this police officer.

On the wrong side of the law in a family dispute

When the police take sides in a family dispute, we assume that they are doing so to protect the real victims. In a shocking case of neglect and abuse, Carby-Samuels had been denied access to his invalid mother, for whom he had been acting in the capacity of a caregiver.

What terrible thing had Mr. Raymond Carby-Samuels done? He had certainly disparaged his father's neglect of his ill wife, Dezrin Carby-Samuels, a step any right-thinking individual would have taken. During the ensuing months when caregiver access was denied to Mr. Raymond Carby-Samuels, and while he attempted to gain adequate care and reasonable access to his mother, the obvious and shocking deterioration in her health spoke of neglect. Worse yet, Mr. Carby-Samuels received a distressing note from his mother, now unable to speak, owing to her condition, in which she alleged that "Dad abuses me".

What police officer in his right mind would support such a state of affairs? As we will see, Detective Griffin is such an officer.

The real victim – justice served?

The level of desperate worry experienced by Carby-Samuels as he frantically tried to regain access to his mother so that she could at least be assured of proper meals while hearing reports from social workers and neighbours regarding Dezrin's rapidly declining condition, can only be imagined. Ms. Dezrin herself, repeatedly requested daily – or at least weekly – access to her son, but being disabled, was unable to leave the family home from which her son had been barred to do so.

Raymond Carby-Samuels turned to the courts in a quest for social justice, and the result of his legal action speaks for itself. The court ordered that Carby-Samuels should be given daily access to his mother to provide her with at least one healthful meal every day. A happy ending? Is justice done? Absolutely! If only Detective Griffin were willing to respect this judgment and cease intimidating Carby-Samuels, while being an accessory to the neglect and abuse of Dezrin.

Threats against Carby-Samuels for taking action

Detective Griffin currently faces charges of assault, battery, and illegal interference laid by Carby-Samuels owing to his continued support of Carby Samuels' father, in excluding Dezrin's son from access contrary to her wishes.

It would be logical to assume that Griffin has 'sided with' Dezrin's husband in a family dispute, despite the court's judgment in favour of Carby-Samuels. Why would a police officer do such a thing? It would be fair to wonder why he is colluding with Mr. Carby-Samuels Sr., in obstructing the ends of justice as reflected in the Court Order. Is there some special relationship between the two men?

Appeal to members of the public

Allowing police corruption to continue is simply not acceptable. Members of the public who may have experienced similar aberrant treatment at the hands of Detective Griffin are asked to step forward, either anonymously, or as witnesses to case 15-SC-13648 against Detective Griffin.

In doing so, they would not only be assisting the cause of justice but also taking action against a rogue cop who is a stain on the otherwise excellent reputation of the men and women of the Ottawa Police Force. Readers who believe they may be of help are asked to contact *The Canadian,* with information, particularly if this relates to witness intimidation and harassment.